The
Happiness Principle
Workbook

A Companion Lesson Manual

Heart Mender Press

Introduction

Welcome to The Happiness Principle Workbook

We want to thank and congratulate you for choosing to participate in The Happiness Principle Program. This workbook is a companion to The Happiness Principle book and will help you apply the angelic teachings found therein. These teachings when learned and consistently applied will change your life and begin to bring true and lasting happiness through an improved relationship with God. There are a few things that are important to understand before you begin this program.

Your HP Guide

This program is most effective when it is initially used under the guidance and care of a Happiness Principle Guide. *What is a Happiness Principle Guide?* It is someone who has already gone through the program and that has seen great success in their own lives as a result. They have then made the decision to spend the rest of their lives helping others attain The Happiness Principle. It is someone who has been trained personally by the authors of the book on how to guide and support others in this quest. They have also been trained in the spiritual healing technique that is discussed in the book. As a result they can help you get more of God's healing light into your life immediately. At some point during each visit they will bless you with more of God's spirit, while easing some of the emotional and spiritual burdens that may be weighing you down.

While you can have sessions on a visit by visit basis, a ten week initial course is available which will really jumpstart your chances for success. During this period your HP Guide can help you with each of the ten lessons in this workbook, and they will get to know you and your problems and will be able to give tailored guidance and advice. Again, you will receive spiritual healing work once a week for ten consecutive weeks which will help to solidly place you on the path to healing and wholeness. Most of all you will be building an important relationship with someone who will always be there during those times when you need a little extra help. Down the road should you go through a personal crisis or a rough patch and need a little extra support, your HP Guide will be there for you. They will be familiar with your situation, have a platform by way of this workbook through which to functionally help you and they will again be able to get more of God's healing spirit to you in such times of difficulty through the spiritual healing work.

While The Happiness Principle concept comes from a place of Christianity, your HP Guide does not promote any particular religion or denomination when they are working in this capacity. They are simply there for one purpose: *To help you make a better connection with God and His blessings, and then to improve upon or grow that connection.* Their support can then be carried over into and should strengthen your own specific religious or spiritual beliefs and pursuits. The concepts and exercises found in this workbook are supportive to most Christian religious beliefs and many other spiritual belief systems.

How to Use This Workbook

To begin, for most of the exercises in this workbook you will need some notepaper or a spiral notebook. The workbook is divided into ten lessons.

Within each lesson you will find *activity boxes*. Participation in the exercises found in some of these boxes is required, while others are optional, while still others are intended simply to inform or uplift.

In Preparation

The *In Preparation* box is the first activity that you will see in each lesson. You are encouraged to complete this activity prior to beginning the lesson. You will be asked to reread the portion of The Happiness Principle that relates to the lesson. You will also be asked to pray about the subject of the lesson and to collect your current feelings and beliefs concerning the topic of the lesson.

In Preparation:

- You will be asked to reread a small portion of the book that relates to the lesson.
- You will be asked to collect your current feelings and beliefs concerning the subject of the lesson.
- You will be asked to focus your daily prayers upon something relating to the subject of the lesson.

Here's an IDEA

The *Here's an IDEA* box contains activities and idea's that provide additional assistance in achieving the goals within the lesson. They are not a required part of the course but are provided for those that would like to put forth a little extra effort within each lesson.

Here's an IDEA:

⇒ Participating in the activities found in these boxes is not mandatory. They are placed here like extra credit exercises. Here you will find activities, exercises and even games that relate to the subject of each lesson. It can be a fun and interesting way to further understand and apply the concepts found in each lesson.

Quotations

The *quotation* boxes are provided simply to uplift and edify. Each box includes a passage from the King James version of the Bible or other quotations that relate to the subject of the lesson. These excerpts can be inspiring and informative and can really add to the strength of the lesson.

"Be kind to yourself
Be patient with yourself
Be forgiving of yourself"

Randy Petersen

Exercises

The *Exercise* boxes are the most important activity boxes, and participation is required. As the name indicates they contain exercises that when diligently and regularly applied will assist in overcoming bad habits, in developing improved character traits and in building a solid foundation for real happiness. Have your HP Guide help you with these exercises.

> **EXERCISE: Introduction**
>
> ♦ When you see this type of activity box, it means that it's time for an exercise that relates to the subject of the lesson.

In this lesson we have learned

The *In this lesson we have learned* box is found toward the end of each lesson and is an encapsulated reminder of what we have just learned.

> **In this Lesson we have learned:**
>
> ✓ This activity box is a reminder of the concepts and information that we have just learned in the last lesson.

MEMORIZE: Personal Precept

The *MEMORIZE: Personal Precept* box contains a percept relating to the concepts that we have just learned about. You are asked to memorize this precept word for word. This activity is required.

> **MEMORIZE: Personal Precept #0 - Introduction**
>
> ♥ This box contains a precept that when memorized will help you remember the concepts that you have just learned.

Additionally

The following two concepts are discussed in The Happiness Principle and we highly recommend that you add them to your program.

The Daily Spiritual Routine

This is the routine that is discussed in the book that provides some time daily for focused and organized spiritual pursuit. While it can be 15 to 30 minutes at any point in the day, morning is an excellent time for this as it helps you get the day started right. This is a great time to pray, do breathwork and spiritual study, and it is the ideal time to refocus on your workbook lessons.

Keeping a Miracle Book

As you see results and begin to make a stronger connection with Father and His blessings, it is very important that you keep a book of remembrance of the signs of His loving influence in your life. As your miracles big and small begin to materialize, write them down and read over these experiences periodically. This is a powerful exercise in which you should participate for the rest of your life. Keeping a miracle book will strengthen your faith in God and will help keep you focused on building a better relationship with Him.

The Purpose of this Workbook

It is very important to understand the nature and purpose of this workbook. The Happiness Principle workbook contains key, foundational truths and concepts that will take time to apply. As a result it is not a course that you go through once and then put away forever. If used properly you will work through this manual again and again, many times throughout your lifetime. These simple yet powerful exercises can be used to improve many areas of your life from bad habits, to character flaws, to relationship issues and the list goes on and on. Of course our ultimate goal is real lasting peace and happiness for ourselves and those we love.

During your initial ten week program you will go through each of the 10 lessons with your HP Guide and while you should see some progress, this will be a time to get familiar with the program and how it works. Once your initial ten week program is complete, you will be instructed to start the workbook all over again from the beginning. This time you'll work each lesson at your own pace. You may spend more than a week on a certain lesson because it's an area in which you need a little extra work. In the future you may skip to a particular lesson in the manual because you feel an immediate need for some help in that area of your life. Be sure to go through the lessons at least twice a year as you continue to build an ever growing personal relationship with God and His many blessings.

Belief and Understanding

- *In this lesson we will focus on developing the concepts of belief and understanding. These principles are foundational in making and maintaining a productive connection with a loving God and His blessings.*

In Preparation:

- Read Teaching One of The Happiness Principle. (pgs. 37-41)
- Focus your daily prayers upon the desire for increased belief and understanding concerning God.
- Ponder upon and collect your current feelings and beliefs concerning God.

Developing Your Belief in God

There is no magic trick for developing a basic belief in God. Belief comes by way of prayer, study, and a real desire to know the truth. While some may search for answers in scientific facts purporting to prove God's existence, a lasting faith and belief is found in an intuitive building of spiritual proof within the heart. It is a gift that is gradually revealed to those that truly desire it and to those that make it a personal priority. Whether you are lacking in belief or you think your belief is strong, the simple act of completing the lessons and exercises in this manual will help to increase belief. Most of this lesson will move beyond basic belief and focus on the character of God. As you develop or strengthen your current belief, an accurate and positive view of Father is essential. If you are struggling with belief then prayer may be an unfamiliar practice to you. If this is true, start out by trying to talk to God. Instead of an eyes closed, head bowed, prayerful approach; go somewhere alone, uninterrupted and talk to God. Eyes open, out load, have a conversation with Him. Ask Him questions, voice concerns, request assistance, and just begin an ongoing dialogue. It must be ongoing because doing this once and then waiting for results will not work. If you will do this once or more every day, in time real belief will start to blossom and a personal connection with Father will begin to be established. These could be the most important conversations you will ever have. If you already have belief you can strengthen that belief through this process or through heartfelt daily prayers that are focused upon the desire for a more certain knowledge of God's existence. This is the most basic foundation for lasting happiness so once you've begun to build it, don't allow anyone or anything to take it from you. Protect your belief like your most valuable possession, and you and your family will receive Father's blessings and care for generations to come.

Here's an IDEA:

⇒ Try to think of family, friends or acquaintances that you know who possess a positive belief in God. Talk to one or more of them and ask them to share the details of that relationship and what it means to them. Use their testimonies to strengthen or begin building your connection with God.

Including God's Positive Character in your Belief

As we have discussed in The Happiness Principle, a basic belief in God is only the beginning. We must view Him as someone who is loving, approachable and that will accept and help us no matter who we are. If we have misconceptions or our impressions are weak then we limit God's ability to assist us with our lives and happiness. The following brief examples have been included in the hope that they might help illustrate how erroneous attitudes concerning God will negatively affect your relationship with Him and your prospects for lasting happiness:

Abandonment

Kari is a young women in her early thirties. While she has never been married, she's had a number of live-in relationships. Kari has three children from two of those partners but is currently single. She has made a lot of poor choices in her life and has faced some real difficulty. While she thinks she has a strong belief in God, she doesn't really spend much time trying to make a better connection with Him. The only time she prays regularly is when she's having major difficulties or is in crisis mode. Then Kari prays and pleads not only for help, but for the outcome that she desires at the moment. Most often her desired outcome is not in her best interest and certainly not part of God's plans so her prayers go unanswered, or so she believes. As a result time and time again, she believes God has abandoned her. Of course if she only knew how often God has protected her and how much more of a disaster her life might be without His assistance, she would not only be astonished but a bit more thankful.

> *"The belief in a God All Powerful wise and good, is so essential to the moral order of the world and to the happiness of man"*
>
> *James Madison*

Here's the problem: If God were an everyday person in her life toward whom Kari had such attitudes, he would be of little help and of little use to her. If she maintained such an attitude toward a family member or friend, in her eyes that person would most likely be unreliable, untrustworthy, and she might even feel contempt toward them because they're not giving her everything she wants and *thinks* she needs. How much positive influence could such a person have in her life? Not much. It is no different with God. Until Kari changes these attitudes and starts trying to get with God's actual plan, her life will continue to be the runaway rollercoaster that she has come to expect.

Here's an IDEA:

⇒ Read stories and testimonials from others that have found a positive relationship with God. Draw strength and inspiration from their experiences, as well as positive character traits from them. Do a web search or go to web sites such as: www.storiesaboutgod.org and gain real belief through these uplifting testimonies. Jump in with both feet and don't look back!

Contempt and Doubt

Chad is 36 years old. He is married and has three children. In the past he has referred to himself as an agnostic but in reality he would probably be more accurately described as antagonistic when it comes to the subject of God. He grew up believing in God but rebelled against that belief as a teenager. As time went on he associated with others that were also opposed to the concept of belief and as a result his contempt for those that believed in an unseen God grew. In recent years his annoyance toward belief has eased but the powerful doubts still remain. His wife recently returned to the religion of her childhood in an attempt to improve their troubled marriage and to help their children who were struggling with behavior issues. After some resistance, Chad agreed to join his wife and children in worship and to participate in helping the family make a connection with Gods love and blessings. Chad now appears to be making a genuine effort for the sake of his family and he has even regained a basic belief in God but the doubts remain strong. He still often wonders why God would allow so many horrible things to happen in this world and why he and his family have suffered so much difficulty at times. Other doubts relating to popular societal teachings that clash with belief, further cloud his spiritual perspective.

"Once you become aware that the main business that you are here for is to know God, most of life's problems fall into place of their own accord."

J.I. Packer

Here's the problem: If Chad continues to allow the outside world and the opinions of his youth to stand as a barrier between himself and God, his positive spiritual growth will be limited. For a while, he should avoid people and influences that feed and strengthen these doubts. Next he should make a personal commitment to fight such negativity when it enters his mind. For the next 90 days if he will act like a believer, soon he will find real, tangible, positive belief.

Unworthiness

Maria is a 40 year old women that holds a deep belief in God. This is supported by the fact that she attends church almost every Sunday without fail. Maria prays multiple times daily and really tries to live a good life. Amidst all of her good works and intentions, Maria suffers from a lingering feeling of unworthiness. Most often when there is a problem in her life, she believes that God is punishing her because she is not living a better life. If she makes mistakes or succumbs to weakness, she tends to focus heavily upon these few occurrences, discounting her many positive qualities. As a result, she feels unworthy of Father's blessings so she will often-times literally refuse to receive them.

Here's the problem: While God blesses Maria in many ways, she is unable and unwilling to receive the fullness of His love and blessings as a result of her mistaken beliefs. Maria must learn that God does not condemn her every time she makes a mistake, but He is there to encourage her to learn from them and grow in that learning. Once she truly begins to believe that God is proud of the many good things that she does and that He loves her unconditionally, she will then be able to stop judging herself so harshly and begin to receive the many blessings that God has waiting for her.

EXERCISE: Increasing Belief

♦ In the exercise on the following page, list your current beliefs or beliefs you've held in the past concerning the character of God. Next list characteristics that improve upon past beliefs or that will overcome these misconceptions. The following examples have been provided to help you better understand this process. Have your *HP guide* help you with this exercise.

EXAMPLE ONE: Perhaps you have suffered a tragedy in life and blamed God for it. Now is the opportunity to mature in those beliefs and correct this destructive pattern of thinking.

Current Belief	Improved Belief
I was mad at God for the death of my dad when I was just 12 years old. I thought that God had abandoned me and my family, and that he didn't care about us.	Now I know that such challenges, although hard, are an opportunity for growth and to rely more on God. My dad is still there, working from the other side on my behalf.

EXAMPLE TWO: You can be a great believer in God and still have mistaken beliefs concerning Him. Maybe you believe in God and feel that He loves you, but you also take a certain amount of pleasure in believing that those that don't share your belief are destined for some kind of purgatory. Here is your chance to eliminate such destructive beliefs.

Current Belief	Improved Belief
I THOUGHT THAT GOD LOVED AND BLESSED ME BECAUSE I HAVE ALWAYS BELIEVED IN HIM. I FELT SPECIAL SINCE I ALSO THOUGHT THAT HE PUNISHED THOSE WHO DIDN'T BELIEVE.	I SHOULD BE ABLE TO FEEL GOOD ABOUT MYSELF AND MY BLESSINGS WITHOUT COMPARING MYSELF TO OTHERS. I WILL PRAY FOR THE WELLBEING OF OTHERS, NO MATTER THEIR BELIEFS.

Improving the Quality of your Belief

On a separate piece of paper or in the spaces provided below, list at least three current or past attitudes or beliefs that you have concerning God. Next list future beliefs you might develop that could help improve upon those attitudes.

1.   **Current Belief**   **Improved Belief**

_____   _____
_____   _____
_____ $\Longrightarrow$ _____
_____   _____
_____   _____

2.   **Current Belief**   **Improved Belief**

_____   _____
_____   _____
_____ $\Longrightarrow$ _____
_____   _____
_____   _____

3.   **Current Belief**   **Improved Belief**

_____   _____
_____   _____
_____ $\Longrightarrow$ _____
_____   _____
_____   _____

Here's an IDEA:

⇒ Now that you have your own list of improved beliefs, take one belief daily and pray upon it. Ask Father to change your heart concerning this issue and improve your belief. Ask Him to reveal His true and loving character to you and to help you begin to build a strong and productive relationship with Him.

In this Lesson we have learned:

✓ That maintaining an unwavering belief in Father is necessary to attaining lasting happiness and personal peace.

✓ That in order to build a productive relationship with Father we must be convinced that He is kind, loving and approachable. That He loves us unconditionally and that He is always trying to extend a hand of help to us in good times and bad throughout our lives.

Doubt is the Enemy of Success

Doubt will slow or even kill growth or progress in any area of our lives. If you have doubts or mistrust in your spouse, then your relationship will most likely languish in mediocrity, rather than being the most productive and rewarding earthly relationship that you have. If you doubt the reliability and vision of your employer, you will be less likely to get excited about your career and won't dedicatedly give it your all. As a result, you will not be well recognized so raises and advancement will be slow to come. But when you believe in something with all of your heart and have a positive vision for the future, then success is more likely. It is no different when it comes to our relationship with God.

When we maintain a strong belief in God without exception, that is when miracles will begin to be seen within our lives. Does this mean that we will never have challenges and difficulties once we've gained such belief? No. In fact the real test of our resolve in this area is during life's greatest challenges and lowest points. If we will get in tune, do those things we've been asked to do, and resist the temptation to start blaming God for our problems but instead stay faithful, that is when we will see his greatest power and favor in our lives. While we will continue to see his hand during the good times, it is during and after life's struggles that we will see not only personal growth but increased growth in our relationship with him, and that is the most valuable blessing of all.

Making a Commitment

Finally, please commit to memory the following precept concerning belief and understanding.

MEMORIZE: Personal Precept #1 - Belief and Understanding

♥ To be truly happy I must believe in a God that is kind, loving and approachable. I know that he loves me unconditionally and is always trying to extend a hand of help to me.

Prayer

- *In this lesson we will focus on developing concepts surrounding prayer. It is the most important component in the pursuit of happiness. Lasting peace and contentment can only be found through daily heartfelt communication with Father. Your goal here is to incorporate the real and functioning power of prayer into your life, and learn how to use this spiritual tool that will produce tangible blessings and positive life results.*

In Preparation:

- Read Teaching nine of The Happiness Principle. (pgs. 90-95)
- Focus on your daily prayers. Pray for the desire to pray regularly.
- Think upon and collect your current feelings and beliefs concerning prayer.

Establishing a Strong Dialogue

While prayer is a personal and intimate form of communication with our Heavenly Father, it is at it's core a real, functioning piece of spiritual machinery. When used and maintained properly, it will deliver actual results. Much like the engine in an airplane, prayer can be a powerful life force that will take you to wonderful places and to heights which you have most likely never before imagined possible. In time as you apply more of the Happiness Principle program within your life, this wonderful process of prayer will become increasingly productive. But much like an engine if certain components such as oil, coolant or gas are missing, the process stops working. This lesson will help you add the necessary components of prayer to your life and fine tune this dynamic spiritual communication tool. We will not be discussing formal, traditional prayer until the end of this lesson, so for now when we use the term "prayer" we are referring to communication with God in a general sense.

The Priorities within Prayer

Lets quickly review the components of prayer as discussed in The Happiness Principle. These points are cornerstones to successful communication with God.

Gods True Character ~ If we believe that Father is anything less than unconditionally loving and concerned, and that He is always working in our best interest, the process of prayer cannot effectively begin.

Relinquish Will ~ It's our own plan that has usually messed things up in the past. Now it's time to let go of our own ego and let God take over. As you pray for a new beginning, a better now or an improved future, you must separate your plan from Father's. Look for patterns in your life that have lead to difficulty in the past, and within the process of prayer strive not to repeat them. Listen for the answer that might not be the easy path but perhaps is the better way. Reject the usual voices that offer instant gratification and more of the same, but instead begin embracing the peaceful prompting that encourages you to do the right thing, perhaps the challenging thing. Remember doing the right thing is not always the easy thing.

"But let him ask in faith, nothing wavering. For he that wavereth is like a wave of the sea driven with the wind and tossed."

James 1:6

Listen and Follow ~ Listening to and discerning Father's promptings takes practice. Here is another area where a strong understanding of the true character of God is helpful. If you are feeling stressed or uneasy concerning the answer you believe you are receiving, it's probably not from God. Of course God may encourage you to take a new and more challenging approach within your life and this can cause some anxiety, but in the end His answers will always be consistent with His character traits and be accompanied by common sense and eventually an overall sense of peace. Once your answer is heard, you must do all that you can to be true to that answer. If you are being asked to take action in a certain area of your life, try to do so with as much consistency, discipline and confidence as you can. Dedicate yourself to the new path that Father has given you and resist any doubts that might weaken your resolve concerning your answer.

Stand Still ~ Now this is the most exciting point in this process, the point after which your blessing will be delivered. It is also where the age old concept of FAITH comes into play. Once you have done all that you have been asked to do, start exercising faith that Father will do the rest. Resist the temptation to become impatient or fearful or to give up. Go about your business, live your life and keep talking to Father. Unless further instructions are received, continue to place it in His hands and don't dwell on it or over think it. If you will do this you will see real answers to prayers. You will see resolutions to problems, advancements in every area of your life, and health and happiness never before dreamed possible.

Let's Talk

In lesson one you were encouraged to begin your quest for belief by talking out loud to God. Here again this approach will be an excellent starting point in establishing or improving upon our daily communications with him. Even if you are a veteran pray-er, you are strongly encouraged to begin by participating in this process. This is something that can be done in addition to prayer. Remember that the author of The Happiness Principle talked to his dad and saw great results so imagine utilizing this process in connection with God. Prayer (which we will cover later in this lesson) is a quiet, solemn practice that is done in a reverent place with eyes closed and mind calmed. Talking to God is a much more dynamic and outward approach that will supercharge your spiritual communications. Try to do it in a focused fashion. Avoid distractions or doing other things while talking to Father. You can sit, walk or pace, but just talk. Ask questions, voice concerns, express gratitude and ask for assistance, and work at opening a respectful dialogue. This may be foreign to some at first but with practice it should become quite comfortable and fluid. Even if you don't see results immediately, keep at it and soon you will. Just like any relationship, the time and effort that you invest is usually representative of how productive and valuable that association becomes. So make your chats with Father one of the most important parts of each day and soon He will show up within your life in a big way.

> ### EXERCISE: Talking to God
>
> ♦ Try to talk to God at least two times daily. Lets begin right now. Wherever you are at this moment, go to a place where you will not be disturbed or overheard. Take a walk, take a drive, just get away for awhile and start talking. Talk to Him as you would a friend. Be open and demonstrative and don't hold back. Make this process a priority. If you only do this once or twice a week it won't work. So make a commitment, make the effort, and make the connection that leads to true and lasting happiness.

The Three Steps of Prayer

So now that we have covered the priorities of prayer and have started an active dialogue with Father, lets look at the steps within the process of prayer that produce real results. There are repetitive statements and request that are included in most prayers. For instance we might ask that our families are protected and kept safe each day. Perhaps we might regularly pray for the wellbeing of people that we don't personally know such as the sick or the poor or those that are suffering from grief. We might pray for the wellbeing of society in general or for our governmental leaders, and we should always include a laundry list of the things for which we are thankful. This said, in most cases our prayers are centered around issues and problems that we wish to personally overcome. Perhaps we are having trouble at work or we are making an important career decision, or we are battling with a personal weakness or addiction, or perhaps we are dealing with problems within our marriage that are causing division and

"And this is the confidence that we have in him, that, if we ask any thing according to his will, he heareth us and… whatsoever we ask, we know that we have the petitions that we desired of him."
1 John 5:14-15

stress. These are the types of personal issues that will be at the center of most of our prayers. Whether it's a sick family member, or a child who is misbehaving, or a poor character trait that we desire to change, these types of personal issues most often are the priority within our communications with God. Now Father wants to guide us to the best resolution to our issue or need, but it is necessary that we hear and embrace the answer that best fits His plan for us. Again we need to separate His guidance from our own personal desires and wants. The three steps of prayer will help us achieve this understanding and make a powerful connection with Father and His blessings.

Step One:

a. ***Pray for Answer*** ~ Of course the first part of this process is to bring your problem or issue before God. Spend some time sharing the details of your situation and ask for guidance and an answer to the problem. If you want something in particular, go ahead and ask for it, but remember that if it isn't part of His plan for you, He probably won't be able to deliver it. Again ask to get in tune with Him and His plan and to receive His will concerning the matter.

b. ***Listen*** ~ While you should continue to talk about your issue in each consecutive prayer, now is the time to start listening for your answer. If this issue is important to you, you will continue to think and ponder upon it. Spend some time each day meditating quietly on the situation and searching your heart for the best resolution.

c. ***What Do You Hear?*** ~ You may begin to hear your answer in this quiet place of meditation or it may begin to come to you in the middle of your everyday life. Either way, begin identifying how you are feeling now concerning your issue. Are you feeling a push or prompting in a particular direction? Are you leaning toward a certain path that might resolve the situation? You might feel peace concerning your problem now and feel you aren't being instructed to do anything. Being patient and having faith might just be your answer. Ideally you should feel strongly about your answer and have an overall feeling of peace surrounding it. If you still feel uneasy about your situation and you are not hearing an answer, go back to the beginning of step one and keep trying. In time you will become more familiar with God's promptings and your answer will come.

Step Two:

a. ***Pray about Possible Answer*** ~ In this step we stop praying about our issue and we start praying about our answer. If you find yourself asking about the issue again in prayer, you may become stalled out in the process. There is no need to further inquire about the original issue because at this point you should be beginning to believe that you have your answer. Now is the time to pray for confirmation of that answer. We do this to make sure that the answer that we have perceived is really coming from Father.

b. ***Receive Confirmation of Answer*** ~ Again after praying, find some quiet time in your day to ponder upon your answer again. You should at this point either begin to feel strongly about your answer or you will be feeling greater doubt. If you are feeling great doubt then you will need to go back to step one and start again. This process can take a little time and effort but it's well worth it. If you believe that your answer is genuine, you should feel confident to proceed.

c. ***Apply Answer and Receive Blessing*** ~ Now all that you have to do is apply your answer. If you believe that it is truly from God then you're in possession of a powerful thing indeed. Make it a priority, give it your all, be consistent and be patient. Pray for strength as you await your blessing. It may not materialize overnight so stand firm in your belief and don't give up. Sometimes things get worse before they get better so exercise a little faith and fight those feelings of fear or hopelessness and just believe. Your blessing is on the way.

Step Three:

a. ***Pray Again and Give Thanks*** ~ Once you begin to see your blessing materialize, you will have real reason to be excited and to rejoice. You will most likely feel a great deal of awe and appreciation concerning a loving Heavenly Father that is real and is there for you. The final step in our process of prayer is to include expressions of thanks within our daily prayers for the blessings that God has given us.

The Prayer Journal

A prayer journal is not as complicated as it sounds. It is not a place where you list everything you prayed about today. Instead it's a way to record the three steps of your personal prayers. Within your prayer journal you can list the thing, issue, person or problem for which you are praying and need help. Next, over time as you pray, list the answers that you are hearing. As you ponder and pray upon these answers, you will have the opportunity to write down your impressions concerning them. As you apply your answer and your blessing materializes, you can record the outcome and your feelings of gratitude. A prayer journal is a way to keep the process of prayer in front of you and in focus.

Here's an IDEA:

⇒ Talk to Father during some of the little breaks in your day. Whether it's right after you drop the kids off at school or after you put them down for a nap, while folding laundry or perhaps on your daily commute to and from work, you can turn these otherwise insignificant periods of time into powerful life changing conversations with God.

Sample Prayer Journal

PRAYER JOURNAL - APRIL 25TH

MY ISSUE OR NEED:

THERE IS INTENSE BICKERING AND CONTENTION BETWEEN MYSELF AND MY HUSBAND RIGHT NOW. IT IS PLACING A STRAIN ON OUR RELATIONSHIP AND WE ARE DRIFTING APART. I NEED TO KNOW HOW TO FIX THIS.

ANSWERS I AM HEARING AND THE ONE I'VE DECIDED TO PRAY ABOUT:

I'M ALWAYS HEARING THAT IF I DON'T FIGHT, HE'LL TAKE ADVANTAGE OF ME. BUT SINCE I'VE BEEN PRAYING I FEEL THAT PERHAPS I SHOULD MAKE A COMMITMENT TO STOP PARTICIPATING IN THE AWFUL FIGHTING NO MATTER WHAT HAPPENS. THIS IS THE ANSWER I'LL PRAY ABOUT.

WHY I BELIEVE I HAVE RECEIVED A CONFIRMATION OF MY ANSWER:

THE MORE I PRAY THE MORE I REALIZE IF I WANT GOD'S HEALING INFLUENCE IN OUR LIVES, I MUST FIRST STOP PARTICIPATING WITH THE DESTRUCTIVE SPIRIT OF CONTENTION.

HOW I PLAN TO APPLY MY ANSWER:

I AM GOING TO RESIST THE TEMPTATION TO BICKER AND INSTEAD TALK TO MY HUSBAND IN A QUIET MOMENT ABOUT MY ANSWER AND SEE IF HE WILL JOIN ME IN FIGHTING THIS SPIRIT OF CONTENTION INSTEAD OF EACH OTHER. I WILL SEE IF HE WILL JOIN ME IN PRAYING FOR PEACE, AND FOR A HAPPY RESOLUTION TO OUR ISSUES AND PERSONAL PRIDE. I'LL TALK TO HIM ABOUT VALUING AND RESPECTING EACH OTHER MORE.

HOW MY BLESSING IS UNFOLDING:

ONCE I STARTED FOLLOWING MY PLAN, THINGS GOT BETTER ALMOST IMMEDIATELY. WE ARE COMMUNICATING BETTER AND WHEN THINGS DO GET HEATED, WE END THE FIGHTING MORE QUICKLY BEFORE HURTFUL THINGS ARE SAID. WE STILL HAVE A WAY TO GO, BUT WE ARE MUCH WARMER TO EACH OTHER AND SOME OF THE ISSUES THAT WE FOUGHT OVER HAVE BEEN RESOLVED WHILE OTHERS JUST DON'T SEEM TO MATTER ANYMORE.

EXERCISE: Prayer Journal

♦ Start your own prayer journal. Over the next couple of weeks pray and journal through one to two issues in your life. Take them one at a time and see each through to the point in which an obvious blessing or improvement has been witnessed.

Proper Prayer

In this lesson so far we have used the term "prayer" a lot but have yet to discuss the actual act of traditional, reverent prayer. Prayer is a wonderful opportunity to make a very personal and meditative connection with Father and should be included in your everyday attempt to build and maintain that relationship. Eventually as your association with Father is more comfortable and fluent, prayer should become the preferred method of communication. We should each participate in our own personal prayer at least once daily. We want to have as many opportunities to stay in touch with Father daily and traditional prayer provides that. You can have daily family prayer as well as prayer between husband and wife. Teaching your children from a young age about Father and His love should be a priority for us all so helping them individually to pray is a great way to start. Saying a blessing at meal time is not near as much about food safety as it's yet another opportunity to reach out and take the hand of God three additional times every day. Now this may sound like a lot of praying but if it is incorporated gradually and is made a priority, in time it will become a powerfully positive habit. The real blessing is the day when we begin to look forward to any opportunity to reach out and make that connection with Father. In the Bible we are encouraged to "pray without ceasing". This too may seem like an impossible task, but as you continue to talk to God and incorporate daily prayers, in time you will find an ongoing internal dialog between yourself and Father throughout each day. As you see things for which you are grateful, you will intuitively give thanks. When you receive guidance or solutions to daily problems you will again find yourself expressing gratitude, and if you need assistance in a moment of difficulty or question, you will automatically reach out for Father's blessings. Remember that communication with Father is the most powerful and important tool in the pursuit of lasting happiness so keep a prayer in your heart and He will overwhelm you and your family with joy, abundance and lasting peace.

In this Lesson we have learned:

✓ To find lasting happiness we must replace our own plan with the plan that a kind and loving Heavenly Father has prepared for us. We must strive to listen and then confirm the answer we have been given. Finally we must have faith, be patient, and do our part.

✓ If putting God first is the priority then we cannot maintain a relationship with Him without prayer. We must strive to improve our communications with Him and find many multiple opportunities to pray each and every day.

Making a Commitment

Finally, please commit to memory the following precept concerning prayer.

MEMORIZE: Personal Precept #2 - Prayer

♥ Praying is one of the most important things that I can do within my day. If I want lasting happiness for my family and myself I must communicate with God every day.

Thankfulness

- *In this lesson we will begin developing and expanding the positive character trait of gratitude within our lives. The power of thankfulness protects and increases God's presence and blessings. Thankfulness is closely partnered with happiness, since it extinguishes the dark emotions of dissatisfaction and discontent.*

In Preparation:

- Read teaching five of The Happiness Principle. (pgs. 61-64)
- Begin to focus on some of the things for which you are personally thankful.
- Ponder upon just how grateful you are right now on a daily basis.

Any relationship is stronger and more significant if a mutual appreciation is shared. Whether it is a family member or friend or coworker, we take better care of those we truly value and of those who value us. Real appreciation usually leads to a true and enduring mutual respect. The same is true with Father. While He loves His children unconditionally, He most likely does not always appreciate or value some of their actions and deeds here upon this Earth. At the same time, many of His children have little appreciation or respect for Him, so there is a disconnect and as a result their relationship with Father is not very productive. Much like an earthly parent is more able to help and guide a child that is thankfully obedient and appreciative, our Heavenly Father is not only much more inclined but much more able to bless us if we possess an ever growing attitude of gratitude. One of the greatest challenges that we face in cultivating such an attitude is found in keeping the valuable blessings that we all have in proper perspective. No matter what is happening in our lives, we can all point to something that is positive and supportive to our wellbeing and happiness. Unfortunately when there are trials and difficulties, our tendency is to focus exclusively upon such challenges and to lose sight of our many blessings. Over time as this process repeats itself, our attitude and focus is shifted toward what's not working out, rather than what has already worked out. An overall attitude of negativity and thanklessness is formed rather than one of hope and appreciation. The good news is we can use thankfulness as a tool to more quickly overcome our problems and stay in a more peaceful and positive place while dealing with life's challenges. To illustrate imagine that your spouse has been in an automobile accident. While there were no injuries you are now faced with a $500 insurance deductible in order to get the car fixed. As you sit at home you stew over the fact that money has been tight lately so this expense plus the cost and hassle of arranging for other transportation during the repairs has you boiling. On top of it all, you learn that your spouse was at fault in the incident and this has you wondering why nothing ever goes your way.

Now while you're wrestling with all of this, across town another man faces a situation much like your own. His wife has also been in an accident and while he faces similar insurance and financial issues, his worries and concerns lie elsewhere. You see his wife was not as fortunate as your spouse, as she was seriously injured in the

> *"O give thanks to the Lord, for He is good; For His loving kindness is everlasting."*
>
> *1 Chronicles 16:34*

crash. Interestingly, this man is not stewing upon insurance, transportation or money problems, but instead is worrying about whether the love of his life will recover from this incident. For this man all of the concerns he had earlier in the day have vanished and now he is worried about only one thing; will his wife recover? While tragic and a little dramatic, this story is included to help you understand that no matter what is happening in your life, there are usually great blessings for which to be thankful and that if we will stay appreciative and focused on those blessings during the tough times, we will be placing Father in a better position to help us. So if you're spouse is in an accident, the better response is absolute relief that they are ok and a belief that the rest will work itself out in time, with Father's help. When we are thankfully positive and hopeful, we attune to those spiritual energies that lead us to Father's guidance, peace and continued blessings but if we are thankless and negative we attune to something that will continue to deliver more issues, more problems and more stress into our lives.

Looking on the Bright Side

It is the age old concept of "The Bright Side". You're probably familiar with it but you may not have known how much power it carries. During at least one of life's challenges we have all heard someone ask us to look on the bright side, encouraging us to focus on our blessings rather than our troubles. Now if you are like most, you briefly entertain such suggestions like a tired old cliché and then you promptly resume stewing and worrying over your problems. But what if the next time you face a challenge, instead of dismissing this idea, you actually took it seriously and gave it a try? And what if you tried this approach to your problems more than once and you began to see results? And what if in time this became a powerful personal character trait that made you a thankfully optimistic problem solver instead of a worrying, pessimistic stresser? After all, the

"We would worry less if we praised more. Thanksgiving is the enemy of discontent and dissatisfaction."

Harry Ironside

whole approach carries with it a powerful message. That is if when facing difficulty you are not looking on the bright side then you must be focusing on the dark side. Those that are truly happy and successful in this world, always focus on their blessings. They value them, they care for them, and in difficult times they look to them as proof that more will soon be on the way.

Challenges are an opportunity to increase our grateful attitude by allowing Father to show His presence in our lives. By staying in tune with Him through the power of thankfulness, He will guide us through any problem or issue and we will come out better and more blessed than before. As Pastor Joel Osteen so perfectly puts it, *"Don't talk to God about how big your problems are. Talk to your problems about how big your God is."*

Here's an IDEA:

⇒ Gather family and friends around the table some evening for an exciting game of Pictionary, but with a twist! Instead of drawing movie titles and the usual Pictionary fare, each person draws something for which they are grateful! The same rules apply (a 60 second time limit, no words, letters, or numbers, when a word is guessed play goes to the other team, etc.) You can use the regular Pictionary board game set, or just grab a pad and paper and enjoy drawing and guessing.

EXERCISE: The Bright Side

♦ This exercise is appropriately called "The Bright Side". List at least three problems or issues in your life about which you are currently concerned. Next for each problem, list a blessing or blessings that will shift your focus to the positive while you are working to overcome these challenges. Have your HP guide help with this exercise.

EXAMPLE ONE: Let's start out with something simple. Imagine that money is tight right now and your washing machine breaks down.

Issue or Problem	The Bright Side
The washing machine is busted and we don't have the money or time to replace it right now. Life is so busy, I don't know when I'll find time to do all this laundry at a Laundromat.	I'm thankful we can afford a used unit until we can buy a better one. Until then I'm blessed that I can use the time at the Laundromat to get away, relax and do some reading.

EXAMPLE TWO: Imagine that the company for which you have worked for over eight years has been hit hard by the struggling economy and has announced that it must downsize. Soon there will be layoffs and no ones job is off limits. You fear that you might lose your job soon and because of the historical recession, you're not sure how long it will take to find work.

Issue or Problem	The Bright Side
I AM CONCERNED THAT I WILL BE LAID OFF SOON. I AM ANGRY WITH MY COMPANY AND FEARFUL FOR MY FAMILY. I'M NOT SURE THAT I CAN FIND A NEW JOB IN THIS ECONOMY.	I WILL BE THANKFUL THAT MY FAMILY IS HEALTHY AND HAPPY. EVEN IF WE HAVE TO CUTBACK FOR A WHILE, THIS MAY BE FATHER'S WAY TO GUIDE ME TO AN EVEN BETTER OPPORTUNITY.

Find the Bright Side to your Problems

On a separate piece of paper or in the spaces provided below, list at least three of the problems or concerns that you are facing right now. Next list blessings and thankful attitudes that you might develop that will shift your focus from your concerns to a more positive outlook.

1.   **Issue or Problem**   **The Bright Side**

_____

_____

_____ $\Longrightarrow$ _____

_____

_____

2.   **Issue or Problem**   **The Bright Side**

_____

_____

_____ $\Longrightarrow$ _____

_____

_____

3.   **Issue or Problem**   **The Bright side**

_____

_____

_____ $\Longrightarrow$ _____

_____

_____

Here's an IDEA:

⇒ Now that you have The Bright Side to at least three of the issues that you are currently facing; why not memorize them? They can be recited like positive counter-points. In the future when you're facing these problems recall The Bright Side. Use them as a shield against the destructive spiritual energies of worry, fear and hopelessness.

Count your many Blessings

Composer Johnson Oatman, Jr. lived between 1856 and 1922 and was famous for writing over 5000 gospel hymns, many of which are included in most church hymnals to this day. In one of his most famous songs entitled "When Upon Life's Billows" he encourages us to count our many blessings.

"When upon life's billows you are tempest tossed, when you are discouraged thinking all is lost, count your many blessings name them one by one, and it will surprise you what the Lord hath done.

Count your blessings name them one by one. Count your blessings see what God hath done. Count your blessings name them one by one. Count your many blessings see what God hath done."

In fact beyond The Bright Side lies the ability to notice and count many, if not most of our most valuable blessings on a daily basis. From the time you first open your eyes in the morning do you look around and notice that you have a home around you that has kept you safe, secure and comfortable throughout your night's slumber. When you walk over to the light switch and flip it on, are you thankful for the instant illumination that you enjoy and the fact that you're not having to fumble for matches and an oil lamp like those that lived just a few generations ago. Do you think about how your clothes and dishes are washed automatically, and no matter what model you own, you have a car that takes you just about anywhere with ease and in comfort. Do you have a job? Well even if your not happy with it; isn't it great that you have income and a way to support your family? And what about the important people in your life; your family, friends and those who care about you? While you love them, do you think about how grateful you are to have them in your life? And are you exercising this level of gratitude each and every day? Now after reading this you might feel exhausted thinking that such a daily approach would be impossible to achieve, but with a little time and focus it is not just doable but very rewarding. From the choice parking space that greeted you at the grocery store to the beautiful sunny day that follows the storm to the wonderful evening you had last night just playing with and loving your kids, if you will learn to briefly ponder each of your many gifts when they occur and give thanks, something wonderful will begin to happen. In time as you become proficient in your daily appreciation it will become harder and harder to be discontent for any extended period of time. It will also help shift your wants and desires from the superficial and spending your hard earned money on things that you don't need. Finally it will help you in identifying more of the true blessings with which God is currently trying to bless you. So let's start counting our many blessing; this can be done by starting a Gratitude List.

> *"He is a wise man who does not grieve for the things which he has not, but rejoices for those which he has."*
>
> *Epictetus*

Gratitude List

The Gratitude List is an exercise designed to shift our focus from a negative problem oriented attitude, to one of gratefulness, and appreciation. Begin by listing at least ten things for which you are thankful. Try to include some of the most important things in your life such as your spouse, children, parents or other important family members or friends. List any positive thing that is important to you and makes life worth living. Next add at least one thing that you are thankful for each day. Then as the list builds, read over the previous days entries before adding new ones. The following sample Gratitude List will give you a better idea of how this process works, and again, the whole exercise can be done using a basic spiral notebook.

Sample Gratitude List

GRATITUDE LIST- MAY 6TH - 20TH

1. I AM THANKFUL FOR GOD & ALL OF HIS LOVE AND BLESSINGS.
2. I AM THANKFUL FOR MY LOVING WIFE AND ALL THAT SHE DOES.
3. I AM THANKFUL FOR MY BEAUTIFUL CHILDREN.
4. I AM THANKFUL THAT WE ARE ALL HEALTHY
5. I AM THANKFUL THAT WE HAVE PLENTY TO EAT & WE'RE NOT NEEDY.
6. I AM THANKFUL FOR THE NICE HOME IN WHICH WE LIVE.
7. I AM THANKFUL FOR OUR COUNTRY & THE FREEDOMS WE ENJOY.
8. I AM THANKFUL FOR THE FELLOWSHIP OF OUR FRIENDS & FAMILY.
9. I AM THANKFUL FOR OUR CHURCH & IT'S FELLOWSHIP & TEACHINGS.
10. I AM THANKFUL THAT I AM BECOMING MORE KIND & PATIENT.

MAY 7 - I AM THANKFUL FOR THE ASSISTANCE THAT I RECEIVED DURING MY PRESENTATION AT WORK. I COULD FEEL GOD'S PRESENCE AND GUIDANCE. I AM BLESSED BECAUSE IT WENT VERY WELL.

MAY 8- I AM THANKFUL FOR THE KIND MAN WHO HELPED MY WIFE WITH A FLAT TIRE AT THE GROCERY STORE TODAY. I AM THANKFUL THAT SHE MADE IT HOME SAFE AND SOUND.

MAY 9 - I AM THANKFUL THAT MY SON SEEMS A LITTLE MORE FOCUSED ON HIS HOMEWORK THIS WEEK. SINCE HE'S STRUGGLED FOR MOTIVATION IN THE PAST, IT'S NICE TO SEE HIM EXCITED AND LOOKING FORWARD TO HIS STUDIES FOR A CHANGE.

MAY 10 - I AM THANKFUL FOR THE BEAUTIFUL DAY THAT WE ENJOYED TODAY. IT'S BEEN KIND OF A HOT AND UNCOMFORTABLE SPRING, BUT TODAY WAS PARTLY CLOUDY AND IN THE LOW 70'S... JUST PERFECT!

MAY 11 - I AM THANKFUL FOR THE WONDERFUL DAY AT THE BEACH THAT WE ENJOYED AS A FAMILY. WE HAD SO MUCH FUN AND EVERYONE STAYED SAFE. WE ALL CAN'T WAIT TO DO IT AGAIN!

EXERCISE: Gratitude List

♦ Start out listing ten of the most important things in your life for which you are thankful. Next add a new entry daily for at least two weeks. List something new that you have noticed in your life or that happened that day for which you are grateful. Read over your list or even recite it out loud after each new entry. A gratitude list will begin to shift you into the habit of noticing & giving thanks for all of your many blessings every day.

In this Lesson we have learned:

✓ That a grateful attitude is necessary to place us in tune with Father and his guidance, and that by learning to look for The Bright Side during times of difficulty, we will be using gratitude as a powerful tool in overcoming our challenges and receiving more of the love, abundance and lasting joy that God has waiting for us..

✓ That we must begin to cultivate a truly grateful character by learning to appreciate all of our blessings throughout each day and intuitively give thanks for them when they occur, and that this is yet another dynamic way to reach out to and connect with Father daily.

The Treasure of Thankfulness

Thankfulness and optimism are like two peas in a pod just as gratitude and positivity are kindred spirits that will light your spiritual road ahead. In time they produce greater hope for the future and a stronger faith in Father. If we teach this powerful attribute to our children, they will be more likely to develop a hopeful "can do" attitude and it will help to bring their priorities inline with Father's.

Many look for happiness through pursuits of pleasure or advancement in career, or in accumulating wealth and belongings, and some believe they will finally be content if they gain control over their world and those around them. Some of these activities can delivery temporary fulfillment, but they most often lead to pain and personal suffering in the end. If your life is built on money and things, all it takes is one moderate economic downturn to end your happiness. Accumulating the treasure of thanks in your heart is the only way to real and lasting happiness. Not just appreciation for the things that you have but for the good people in your life, and the truths that you're learning and the growing peace in your heart. Don't be satisfied with what you have but be thankful for what you have and then, by way of your growing relationship with Father, more will come in a balanced and healthy fashion.

Making a Commitment

Finally, please commit to memory the following precept concerning thankfulness.

MEMORIZE: Personal Precept #3 - Thankfulness

♥ I will try to look at The Bright Side in every situation and to give thanks for all of the blessings big and small found along life's path daily.

The Meaning of Life

- *In this lesson we will have the opportunity to analyze what life's meaning and purpose is to each of us. Then we will look at how that purpose compares to God's plan and how we might make adjustments to bring it more in line with His purposes.*

In Preparation:

- Read teaching three of The Happiness Principle. (pgs. 52-56)
- Begin to focus on why you believe you are here in this life and what you are here to accomplish.
- Pray for desire and assistance in aligning your purpose with God's plan.

While determining life's personal meaning is up to each of us, its overall purpose is important to understand so that we might build our lives around it. It makes a certain amount of sense that if we want to come closer to God then understanding and participating in His program is a must. So prior to reading The Happiness Principle; did you ever contemplate why you are here on this planet? When you wake up each day, what is the main motivator in your life? You might answer, "I love my career! I live for it and what it provides me". Perhaps you might say, "I live to ski!" or "All I work for is the weekend when I can party!" What is that first thought that comes into your mind each day that drives you forward? Do you have goals? What are they? And where do you think they will have you in the next ten years? Perhaps you believe that you are doing a wonderful work from which many benefit daily. Or maybe your first thoughts each day are negative in nature. "Oh I can't believe I have to get up and face another day." " I really hate my life and wish it were different." If you live in such a state of negativity and you could magically change your life; in what way would you change it? When you consider what you live for or how you wish your life could be, you will discover much of your view on what life's meaning is to you.

> *"The sole meaning of life is to serve humanity."*
>
> *Leo Tolstoy*

If you were to sit down and write a couple of paragraphs detailing why you do what you do every day, what would it say? Would it resemble God's plan at all? Remember that Father's work and main priority is the spiritual growth and well-being of His children. Perhaps your main priority is your children. This is a wonderful answer. Now if you were asked to write a couple of paragraphs roughly outlining where you hope all of your hard work will have your children in the next 15 to 20 years; where would that be? Who do you hope they will become? Will their lives mesh at all with God's overall plan? While some of us set goals or have a general idea of our aspirations, most go through life being driven solely by their passions and desires, rarely contemplating the big picture. This picture is the view of where today's choices will lead us in the future. Will it be the image of joy and personal peace or one of broken hopes and dreams, of happy and united personal relationships, or one of divorce and broken homes? Will it feature health and prosperity or dysfunction and struggle? But how can we gain such a view of the future? It can be done by taking a snap shot of what life represents to each of us today. So again, what drives you forward each day? What is the legacy you wish to leave behind for your family, for your children, for the world? Why are you here? What have you come here to do? Who have you come here to be?

Life's Meaning Examined

Socrates said, "A life unexamined is not worth living". It might also be said that one's purpose in this world left unexamined may not be worth living either; so hey, let's examine it. Remember in elementary school when the teacher asked you to write an essay? She would give you a topic about which she wanted you to write, in no less than 150 words. Well the next exercise will encourage you to do just that. The topic will be "What is life's purpose or meaning to you and how are you striving to fulfill that purpose each day?" Now if your name is Ralphie and your only goal and purpose in this world is to obtain a BB gun then this will be easy for you, but for the rest of us it may take a little more thought. Hopefully the following examples will help you understand and better prepare for this exercise. As you read these examples keep in mind that an important part of this process is to not only write this essay but to then try to identify ways you can bring your current lifestyle and purpose more inline with God's purposes. If you have children, be sure to include the role that they play in your view of life's purpose.

"Flee also youthful lusts: but follow righteousness, faith, charity, peace, with them that call on the Lord out of a pure heart."

2 Timothy 2:22

Example One: Julia

Julia is 38 years old, is married and has four children ages 5-13. She is a stay at home mom that proudly proclaims that her children are her life. This is proven by the fact that she is on the run from sports practices and music lessons and dance classes throughout the week. She believes that if she keeps her kids busy they will stay out of trouble. She often says that she has pretty good kids compared to most. They belong to a church which they attend a few times a year. Julia and her husband have a distant but at times warm relationship. With the exception of an occasional blow up, they have learned to manage their differences, animosities, and resentments for the sake of the kids. This is her essay:

What life's meaning and purpose is to me and how I strive to fulfill that purpose each day

I believe that life is what you make it. I think I am here to raise my children and make them successful. I think the best way to see my philosophy is to look at what I try to teach my kids. I am here to teach them about the realities in life and to help them avoid the mistakes that I made. I teach my kids that they should be kind to others but that they should not allow themselves to be taken advantage of. It's nice to think about helping the other guy, but the truth is that life is a competition and the best way to help others is to become the best you can be.

I believe one of life's top priorities is becoming educated and prepared. I teach them to graduate from college and try to find out who they are before they ever think about starting a family. I teach them to be environmentally conscious and socially aware. I stated in the beginning "life is what you make it" and in the end the only person you can truly rely upon is yourself so you'd better make that person the priority and you'd better make them the best they can be.

A Closer Look at Julia's Essay

Well you have to give Julia credit for her honesty. She makes no bones about her purpose and the role that her children play in it. While we find within her stated purpose some great and honorable things, we also find that some key components are missing. It's true that the precepts that she teaches her children are practical and certainly useful in the temporal world, but they are not of much help on a spiritual level. What she believes in and teaches is reliance upon one's self and upon educational institutions and no one else. If focus upon God and His plan is the true path to happiness, then she may be preparing her children for failure and disappointment. A lack of focus upon Father is most likely the cause of Julia's own unresolved struggles and resulting jaded perceptions. As a result she now teaches a defensive strategy to her children concerning life and their future, devoid of any mention of God. Just as the existence of God is obviously missing from her essay, her husband too is suspiciously absent. Due to the couple's past issues and problems, she has relegated him to a necessary but untrustworthy and unreliable component. He has never been able to completely get on board with her program and maintains views that differ from her own. This she has not let get in her way, as she knows what's best for the children and their future. God has a lot in common with her husband in this regard as when she did go to church regularly with her parents years ago, the will of God as she perceived it never really agreed with her views and beliefs concerning life.

To anyone that has read The Happiness Principle, some of the problems within Julia's beliefs should be glaringly apparent. The first problem of course is that God has been completely removed from the equation. Replacing Father with a total and complete reliance of one's self or those that agree with us, is flawed from the start. Look at all of the various beliefs and approaches out in the world. From those that are striving to become great political or social leaders to those that pursue nothing but pleasure and thrill, to those that advocate relentless bloody war, to those that promote naïve, doe-eyed peace through surrender, to the woman who is addicted to alcohol, to the man that is addicted to pornography, to the boy who is obsessed with video games, to the workaholic woman that is driven day and night to endlessly achieve. Many of these people have also been taught to believe in themselves, to be true to themselves and what they want and desire, and as a result the things in which they believe must always be right. What dwells within us and the spiritual energies to which we are connected do not always lead us to our best possible life and rarely lead to real happiness.

Julia must first personally develop a genuine belief in God and then cultivate a relationship with Him. As soon as this connection has become functional, she should begin to shift her children's reliance on self to reliance upon and faith in God. While education and many of the other things she is guiding them toward are worthwhile, they can also be dangerous and destructive in a spiritual sense without Father's guidance. With God's help she must also work toward healing the relationship with her husband so that in time their children will see that a loving and committed partnership between an man and a woman is supportive to lasting happiness instead of just a component that is selfishly used to gain personal success.

> ### Here's an IDEA:
> ⇒ Once you have written your essay, come back in 6 months to a year & do this exercise again. Without looking at your last essay, write a new one. Once you have finished compare it to your previous writing & see how much your attitude concerning life's purpose and meaning has changed.

Example Two: Lewis

Lewis is a 27 years old mechanic. His most recent live-in girl friend has been with him for two years and together they have a baby girl who is just ten months old. His girlfriend wants to get married but Lewis is very resistant. His parents have been married and divorced multiple times so he just doesn't believe in it. This has been a point of contention but she loves him and now because of their child she feels an even greater bond. Lewis has consented to go through the Happiness Principle program with her if she'll agree to drop the marriage talk for awhile. She hopes that it will help him shift his priorities more toward her, the baby and eventually a greater level of commitment.

> *"A life directed chiefly towards the fulfillment of personal desires sooner or later always leads to bitter disappointment."*
>
> *Albert Einstein*

Lewis works to play! If he's not at his shop then he is out on the lake boating with his friends or dirt biking or fishing or hunting and many other outdoor activities. While he is generally pleasant and seemingly happy, he suffers at times with periodic bouts of depression. Eventually it became so bad he was put on a medication that he now takes regularly. It helped at first but over time he has gradually slipped back into a similar cycle of depression. His girlfriend has encouraged him to shift his focus to God in an attempt overcome this destructive cycle, but he believes that he gets depressed because he's not active enough and so as soon as he can, he renews the focus upon his real passion... recreation. Lewis' girlfriend feels stuck in an empty and quite often meaningless cycle of partying and depression. She feels like if there were an opportunity to leave the relationship, that chance has passed since they now share the connection and responsibility of their beautiful daughter. Lewis is resistant to change and almost habitually opts for more of the same. This is his essay:

WHAT LIFE'S MEANING AND PURPOSE IS TO ME AND HOW I STRIVE TO FULFILL THAT PURPOSE EACH DAY

LIFE IS TO BE LIVED. YOU'RE EITHER A SPECTATOR OR A PLAYER AND I AM DEFINITELY A PLAYER. I THINK WE ARE ALL HERE TO FIND OUR OWN BRAND OF HAPPINESS AND THAT'S EXACTLY WHAT I'M DOING. I TAKE PRIDE IN MY WORK AND I'M GOOD AT IT, BUT THAT'S NOT WHAT DEFINES ME. IT IS THE THINGS THAT I DO OUTSIDE OF WORK THAT MAKE LIFE WORTH LIVING. I PLAY HARD AND LOVE LIFE AND THAT IS ALL YOU NEED TO BE HAPPY.

WHILE I AM FIRST AND FOREMOST A LONER, MY GIRLFRIEND AND BABY GIRL HAVE ADDED TO MY JOY AND NOW I DON'T KNOW WHAT I WOULD DO WITHOUT THEM. I GET DOWN NOW AND THEN BUT I THINK THAT'S JUST LIFE AND SOMETHING I HAVE TO LIVE WITH. IF YOU FALL OFF THE HORSE, YOU JUST HAVE TO TRY TO GET BACK ON IT. THERE'S NOT MUCH ELSE YOU CAN DO.

A Closer Look at Lewis' Essay

In the past Lewis has joked that the great outdoors is his God, and the forests, lakes and streams are his church. Unfortunately mother nature has not delivered lasting peace of mind and happiness to Lewis, or his girlfriend for that matter. His superficial approach to life and his avoidance in dealing with problems and issues from the past has trapped him and his new little family into a slowly sinking spiritual state, that will most likely end in a broken home with all of the accompanying hardships.

Of course the only lasting deliverance from his methodic downward spiral is a conscious and consistent effort to connect with God and His healing light and guidance. While Lewis will be able to continue his love affair with the great outdoors, a connection with Father will provide the answers and assistance needed to protect such passions, not to mention his girlfriend and daughter. Once he has made that connection and is seeing some personal progress, eventually he will need to ponder an important decision that probably should have been considered prior to the conception and birth of his child. Is his girlfriend that one important person that can support him and love him throughout the rest of his life, and can he do the same for her? If so then he should provide her and their baby with the commitment that they deserve and then he should get to work honoring it. With this ever shifting focus and change of values, hopefully in time one of Lewis' future essays will be a little less self serving, include a mention of God, and place his daughter and girlfriend a little higher on the list than his personal pastimes and amusements.

> ### EXERCISE: Essay: Life's Meaning
>
> ♦ Now its your turn to write an essay entitled: **"What life's meaning and purpose is to me and how I strive to fulfill that purpose each day"**. It should be no less than 150 words and no longer than a single notebook page. If you have children, be sure to include the role that they play in your view of life's purpose. Read your finished essay to your HP Guide so they can lead you through this process. Share your thoughts with them on how you might bring your current lifestyle and purpose more inline with God's purposes.

Adding Meaning to Your Purpose

So now that you have been helped in indentifying where you may be off track concerning your overall purpose in this life, the next simple step is to quickly make the necessary adjustments and "presto change-o" you're set, right? Well, probably not. Most of us for years have been driven by passions, wants, desires and appetites, so our current overriding purpose and drive may not shift so quickly. But if we will keep the results of this little exercise in mind and strive daily to make the shift, in time our entire perspective on life's meaning will change for the better.

In this Lesson we have learned:

✓ If our purpose is out of alignment with Father's purpose and path for us, then we are most likely heading down a dead end street. By making the necessary corrections, in time our true purpose we lead us and those we love to real and lasting happiness and fulfillment.

Making a Commitment

Finally, please commit to memory the following precept concerning life's purpose.

MEMORIZE: Personal Precept #4 - Life's Purpose

♥ I will remember that I am not only here to bless myself but to be a blessing to others. So I will make God's purpose and plan a part of my purpose and plan.

Priorities & Moderation

- *In this lesson we will take a look at our current priorities and how they stack up next to those things that are important to Father. Then we will try to find greater balance within those priorities and the regular activities and routines they tend to create.*

In Preparation:

- Read teaching seven of The Happiness Principle. (pgs. 75-85).
- Begin to focus on which things are of greatest importance to you in life.
- Pray for desire and assistance in aligning your priorities with God's plan.

No matter who you are, you have a list of priorities by which you live. They may not be written down, or you may not have ever consciously thought about them for that matter, and yet they do exist for each of us. From the guy down the street who is so focused on career and advancement, he can be seen leaving for work six sometimes seven mornings a week. To the lady across the way who spends all of her daylight hours working in her flowerbeds and garden. To the 28 year old man that lives in his parents basement in the house behind you and with the exception of an occasional break in the backyard to smoke pot, does nothing but watch TV and surf the internet every day. Whatever they may be we all have things that are important to each of us which we consider priorities.

In parable Jesus compares the priority of God and His kingdom to a man who when he discovered a treasure hidden in a field, went quickly and sold everything that he owned so that he could purchase that piece of land. He also compared the kingdom of heaven to a merchant that was seeking fine pearls and when that man found one pearl unmatched by any other, a pearl of great price, he sold all that he had in order to possess it. Here again we find the very essence of The Happiness Principle as Jesus confirms that there is great power in putting Father and his purposes ahead of all other priorities in our lives. But which of us is willing or able to make such a level of commitment? To forsake all and dedicatedly follow Father in everything that we do? It's a tall order.

> *" Lay not up for yourselves treasures upon earth, where moth and rust doth corrupt, and where thieves break through and steal: But lay up for yourselves treasures in heaven"*
>
> *Matthew 6:19-20*

After all most of us are ensconced in responsibilities, schedules and priorities that we have been managing for years. Much of it we do for the betterment not only of ourselves but for the wellbeing of our families and loved ones. Our lives usually represent a long term investment in something, whether it be a career or a passion. It would be hard to have the faith necessary to abandon it all, so that we might focus solely on things spiritual. Perhaps instead of trying to change all of our priorities all at once, we could start by trying to include Fathers plan within our current list of daily priorities. With the exception of activities that clearly do not serve ourselves or our families well, Father's purposes can be incorporated into almost any daily activity. So now you may ask, how can I bring God's purposes into my work day, or into my football practice, or while I'm watching TV, or working on my car? Well let's find out if it's possible.

Realizing Our Priorities

Before we join God's priorities with our own, we must first identify the things we do most days; the things that makes life worthwhile for each of us. The things that in reality, are our actual personal priorities. The following exercise will be done in two parts. In the first part we will list those main daily or weekly pursuits that make up our lives and then finally we will find ways to include God's plan and priorities within those pursuits. The following example will help you understand how this is done.

> *"The key is not to prioritize what's on your schedule, but to schedule your priorities."*
>
> *Stephen R. Covey*

Improving Our Personal Priorities - Example One:

So say your average day consists of getting up, having breakfast, getting the kids off to school, going to work and coming home, having dinner, doing a few chores around the house, helping your children with their home work, watching some TV, surfing the internet for a while, doing a little reading and then going to sleep. While your weekday schedule changes slightly now and then as you go out to eat sometimes or go to a movie, etc., most of the time it remains the same. On the weekend your schedule changes a little as you have a more free time. Usually it involves additional household chores, sporting events, and outings involving swimming or going to the zoo or the park, or a number of other activities.

Part One:

In the first part of this exercise simply list these daily activities. Only list weekend activities if it is something in which you participate most weekends. So the above example might look like this:

**IMPROVING PERSONAL PRIORITIES
PART ONE**

DAILY	WEEKEND
- BREAKFAST	- CHORES
- KIDS TO SCHOOL	- SWIMMING
- WORK	
- DINNER	
- CHORES	
- HOMEWORK	
- WATCH TV	
- INTERNET	
- READING	
- BED	

Part Two

In the second part of this exercise we take a few of the activities from the priority list that we just made and think of ways to add Father's priorities to them. While this may be challenging to do with some activities, with most it can be accomplished. So let's take our first example which is getting up in the morning. In the past you may have showered, grabbed some coffee, read the newspaper or surfed the internet. How about adding a spiritual routine to your morning? Just 10 to 15 minutes that include prayer, breath work and some reading will start your day out right by focusing on Father and His priorities. Next while at work you might help a struggling coworker with ideas and techniques in accomplishing their weekly

> *"For where your treasure is, there will your heart be also."*
>
> *Matthew 6:21*

work quota. Perhaps you are struggling to find time in your busy schedule to spend more quality time with your spouse. How about setting up a fun lunch date in the middle of the workday and grab a little alone time. From our sample list the next activity that you might want to focus upon is dinnertime. Maybe you usually have the TV on during dinner. Why not turn it off and talk as a family? How about making a blessing over the food at dinnertime a priority? After dinner when it's times to watch a little TV, how about instead of just always watching what's on, plan some family programming. Gather your family around and put on some classic and clean family TV or movies. Watch something now and then of a faith based or spiritual nature. If you read a little before bed, why not include a book of a spiritual or character building nature on your night stand? Include such a book every other or third book that you read. If you do extra chores on the weekend, how about turning Saturday morning into a family chore party. Turn on some fun music and do your chores together. Dance, sing and turn what can usually be drudgery into a fun family event. Perhaps you go to the lake for boating and swimming most Sundays in the summer. Why not go a little later and spend an hour or two at church in the morning. Almost any activity on your schedule can include pursuits that will draw us and our families closer to God and closer to one another.

IMPROVING PERSONAL PRIORITIES
PART TWO

- GETTING UP: TEN MINUTES FOR SPIRITUAL ROUTINE.

- WORK: HELP PAM AT WORK TO FIND WAYS TO COMPLETE WORK LOAD BY END OF THE WEEK.

- DINNER: TURN OFF THE TV AND TALK AS A FAMILY DURING DINNER. MAKE A BLESSING ON THE FOOD A PRIORITY.

- TV WATCHING: GATHER THE FAMILY AROUND AND WATCH SOME CLASSIC TV SHOWS.

- NIGHTTIME READING: INCLUDE SOME SPIRITUAL BOOKS ON THE NIGHT TABLE AND READ ONE EVERY THREE BOOKS.

EXERCISE: Improving Our Personal Priorities

♦ Now its your turn to examine your own personal priorities a little more closely and then try to incorporate some of God's interests into your activities and interests. First: on a separate piece of paper list your daily and weekly activities that make up your real-life priorities. Next: Take a few of those activities and think of ways to incorporate God's purposes within them. Finally: actually put forth the effort to make these changes in your schedule. Over time look for additional ways that you can add God's interests within your own interests. Be sure to have your HP advisor help you with this exercise.

Balance through Moderation

In the book The Happiness Principle, we learn that the path to a balanced life is through moderation. For instance, you can become very rich and successful by working at your career 60 or 70 hours a week. Unfortunately, by investing so much time in just one area, other facets of your life must suffer. If you have a family, they will surely feel the results of your absence and this imbalance can cause long term problems for everyone involved. Another example might be if you played video games all night, almost every night of the week. While subsisting off of fast food and soda pop, you experience little physical activity other than the exercising of your trigger finger. Again we see obvious imbalance here as such an obsessively excessive behavior would lead to imbalance in the areas of poor physical and social health, just to name a few. Of course, the best way to bring greater equilibrium to both examples is through the power of moderation. While the above examples are extreme, we all have areas in our life that could use the blessing of balance that moderation can deliver. There is no organized exercise in this lesson concerning balance and moderation, but it would be wise to take a look at the real life priority list that we just made in the previous exercise and see if there are activities which may be out of balance. For instance you might be a parent that has their children on the run constantly from school to dance to music lessons to soccer practice to a pile of homework to bed to the next day, on and on, over and over again. Perhaps your kids have begged for some of the pressure to be taken off of them, but you know that if they stay busy they will stay out of trouble and all of these activities will help them in their adult lives ahead. But what if you moderated their schedule a little and planned more family activities or just gave them more time to be kids. It's possible that this added balance might benefit them more not only in the future but the present. So look at your list and when you find areas of excess, moderate them. Too much work, add a little leisure. Too much leisure, get to work. Are you stuck in front of the TV most nights? Moderate it. Go visit a friend or family member and brighten their day. Go to the park and shoot some hoops or throw some horseshoes or just take a walk. If you'll mix it up and moderate it, you will find the balance in life that lends itself to real personal peace and of course, happiness.

In this Lesson we have learned:

✓ Our priorities must include God's plan and priorities if we wish to make a lasting connection with Him and His blessings. We must also moderate excesses within our priorities in order to live in a more balanced, healthy and peaceful fashion.

Making a Commitment

Finally, please commit to memory the following precept concerning priorities and moderation.

MEMORIZE: Personal Precept #5 - Priorities and Moderation

♥ I will try to always include God's priorities within my own personal priorities, and I will strive for balance in my life by moderating excesses.

Positivity and the Soul

- *In this lesson we will learn how to strengthen the eternal soul that resides within each of us by incorporating the power of the spoken blessing into our lives and the lives of others. Next we will focus on shifting our conversational patterns into a more hopeful and positive direction.*

In Preparation:

- Read teaching four (pgs. 57-60) and teaching six (pgs. 65-74) of The Happiness Principle.
- Begin to focus on your beliefs concerning the soul and the current state of your own internal and external dialogue.
- Pray for desire and ability to create a more positive and uplifting personal environment for your soul.

The soul within each of us is the essence of who we really are. As discussed in The Happiness Principle, continued positive development of the soul is very important to our long term bliss. In order for the soul to increase it must be encouraged, and fed those things that will add to its overall health. To begin, we must ask ourselves if we actually believe that there is an eternal spirit residing within us. If this is a concept that seems agreeable to you, then it's time to make a more vivid and productive connection with your soul. This component is very special indeed because it's more than just an intelligent spirit. It only becomes a *soul* when it is born and joined with a physical body. From this point forward the hope is that the soul and the conscious physical self will reclaim its true spiritual talents and gifts, and continue developing them for use in God's overall plan. Again as previously discussed, the development of the soul is quite often slowed early in life as a result of unresolved traumas or difficulties. The soul might also be taken off course when the conscious self is drawn into behaviors and desires that are not healthy for our inner spirit and its true purposes. In order for the soul to begin to heal and increase once again, a more positive, balanced and uplifting environment must be created. That environment is the one within our hearts and minds. So rather than an internal environment filled with negatives such as anger, resentment, regret, guilt, worry, or fear, the soul needs hope, positivity and love in order to flourish.

> *"Pleasant words are as an honeycomb, sweet to the soul, and health to the bones."*
>
> *Proverbs 16:24*

Positive Thinking

Many of the positive thinking gurus of our day, approach this subject from the stand point of the subconscious mind. Others focus on the language of the mind and it's affect on the nervous system. Their goal is to assist their students in changing the way they view themselves and others, and the manner in which they instinctively respond to personal issues and challenges. While some of their guidance and exercises can be helpful, at the end of the day most are encouraging their followers to continue to manipulate the physical process of the mind, while relying upon self. One of the greatest obstacles in traditional positive thinking is one of motivation. If you're going it on your own, a lasting result is unlikely for most. But if you involve God in the process and place the focus on the living soul rather than the machine that is the brain or the physiological process that is the nervous system, more enduring results namely happiness will follow.

Empty Affirmations

While there are many psychological and pseudo-psychological approaches that claim to discipline the mind and emotions, one that has been used with great frequency is the *positive affirmation*. It is a brief statement that when, repeated with enough regularity, over time is reported to literally change the way that we think. Affirmations can be positive or negative. When you think about it, most of us have heard these types of thoughts repeating over and over in our minds throughout our lives. We might periodically hear phrases like, "You're stupid" or "That was dumb" or "you mess that up every time". While others might hear, "Hey you're awesome", "Nobody's more good looking than you" or " There is nothing you can't do. You're the best!" Hence these types of thoughts are common to the human mind. Most often affirmations are used to replace negative defeating thoughts with positive uplifting encouragements. This is hoped to change the way that we instinctively think and in time improve the manner in which we live our lives and respond to challenges.

All of this said, affirmations are nothing more than suggestions since most often they have no real basis in our current reality. They are simple encouragements that are used to trick the mind into working in a different and hopefully more productive fashion. Here is a very basic example. Say that you are overweight and you wish to lose a few pounds and get healthy. In addition to exercise, a dietary weight loss plan and other lifestyle changes, you also add some positive affirmations. One of your affirmations might go something like this: *I am a healthy, beautiful, slender person.* Now, while you're most likely a very beautiful person, the truth of the matter is that, at this point in time, you are not very slender and your health just might leave something to be desired.

So an affirmation is simply a conditioning tool that hopes to convince the mind to live in a particular fashion until true results are seen. While affirmations can be helpful, they don't work well for everyone. If you tend to be a confident person then affirmations will probably work for you, but if you are unconfident or even depressed, they can actually make things worse. They must be structured carefully because if they are too outside the realm of reality, the subconscious mind just won't buy them.

There's a better way to change and motivate the mind while engaging not only our own soul and but the souls of those around us by tapping into the greatest power for personal change in the Universe. Instead of the empty promises of affirmations, why not invoke the blessings and majesty of God in our lives. What better way to change character flaws, create lasting optimism and hope, and heal our very souls then to actively call down the power of heaven upon our families, our friends, our places of work, our communities and upon ourselves. Yes instead of affirming the possible, perhaps we should be confirming the unlimited power for growth and healing that awaits us by speaking blessings not only over our own lives but over the lives of others.

Here's an IDEA:

⇒ Instead of affirmations try repeating passages from a sacred text like the Bible from time to time. You can find scriptures relating to healing, hope, courage, faith and much more. Many of these passages are promises made to the faithful over the centuries and as a result they carry with them great power.

The Spoken Blessing

It's important to understand that affirmations are not bad things. Telling yourself that you can do it or that you are strong enough or capable enough to get through the tough times in life can be a valuable thing, but shifting from encouraging phrases to empowering spoken blessings can end up being an absolute game changer. In addition to prayer, when blessings are spoken the soul is awakened and it gets involved. It reconnects with God and that's when the blessings begin to flow. There are two types of spoken blessings: *active blessings* and *everyday blessings.*

Active Blessings

Active spoken blessings are the ones with which you're probably the most familiar. They might be spoken over a person like a laying on of hands blessing or they can be a spoken over a thing like a house or over a situation or a problem. Aside from our own children or a close family member, most of us are not going to have the opportunity to give *active* spoken blessings to everyone around us so for our purposes here, we are going to focus on speaking blessings over situations in our lives. These types of blessings can at times seem similar to affirmations but remember that they can literally carry the power of God within them. The easiest way to explain this concept is by way of a few examples.

" Death and life are in the power of the tongue ."

Proverbs 18:21

The Blessing of Focus

Many of us have struggled with a lack of focus at times throughout our lives. Drifting from productive pursuits to activities that waste our precious time, or experiencing prolonged unmotivated periods can literally steal years of our lives. So in addition to an inspired plan that makes key changes in this regard, spoken blessings can be added to help during those unmotivated periods. A spoken blessing concerning focus might go something like this:

Father has promised me His spirit so His light, understanding and excellent wisdom works through me. He gives me the power to focus and work diligently on the tasks at hand. I can accomplish anything that I have been inspired to do. If God is with me, nothing can stand against me. I bless this day with the power of God's focus, diligence and success!

While you can tailor and word the blessing in your own personal fashion, the above example should give you an idea of how this process works. Blessings can be spoken at anytime but they tend to be of greatest benefit during our moments of weakness. If your working through your day and find yourself unfocused and stalled out, take a walk and repeat your blessing. While you can repeat your spoken blessing multiple times per occasion, try not to become mechanical and automated during this process. Slow down and think about the meaning of each sentence as you say them. Start trying to believe in the content of your blessings and that in time they will come to pass. You may be prompted to add additional lines or concepts to your spoken blessings. In fact, eventually you may begin to speak fully inspired blessings that are composed in the moment. These unscripted, non-repetitive spoken blessings carry with them even greater power as the words can be tailored by angels themselves before they fall from your lips, and can better address the needs of a particular situation in the moment. These types of blessings can be spoken over any character flaw, issue or problem you are striving to conquer.

Blessing for a Wayward Child

During our lifetimes some will face the challenge of an older child that strays from his or her path in life. Whether it be poor lifestyle choices, addictions, destructive behaviors, or simple rebellion, many parents suffer greatly when a child loses their way. During these times a parent will experience periods of great regret and remorse, worry and fear, or even anger. It's hard not to participate in these kinds of dark spiritual emotions when in the midst of such trials but when we do, we are actually slowing the arrival of our blessing and a possible resolution to the problem. Spoken blessings can be used to overcome those dark moments of anxiety and to direct more of God's love and light onto the situation, while strengthening your own hope and faith. A spoken blessing designed to assist a lost or wayward child might go something like this:

> *"A merry heart doeth good like a medicine: but a broken spirit drieth the bones.."*
>
> *Proverbs 17:22*

God has promised to make a way of escape for my child from these behaviors. My job is to find God's plan concerning my child and do my part. It is not my job to worry or complain but to believe. I know that Angels have been sent to guide my child out of this darkness, so with patience and faith I now place their welfare into God's hands. I bless my child and our entire family with God's healing spirit of hope, love and patience in anticipation of this blessing.

You may have noticed that spoken blessings are a great opportunity to not only exercise God's promises, but to remind ourselves of the part we must play in the blessing. It is a chance to recommit daily to the role we have been given if we wish to see a positive outcome. Unlike an affirmation which might keep you a little more positive during such difficult times, a spoken blessing allows you the opportunity to literally direct God's healing love toward your child and your entire family. This type of situation is more challenging than most because it involves the free will of an older, ever changing child. While you might not see the perfect outcome for which you are hoping, you should see some improvement or even a level of resolution as a result of spoken blessings. More importantly, these blessings will help you maintain your personal peace, not to mention your sanity during such trying times.

Blessing the Fight Against Disease

Dealing with a life threatening disease or physical condition can be one of the most overwhelming issues anyone of us will ever face. The fear and uncertainty that attacks the victim as well as their family and friends is indescribable. If you are ever faced with such a situation, regular spoken blessings are a must. The following is just one example of how a blessing aimed at physical healing, namely overcoming cancer might read:

God has promised that He will be with me in trouble and will deliver me. That He will satisfy me with long life if I focus my love upon Him and call upon His name. I will not allow the dark spirit of cancer to take me from my family and loved ones. I command this destructive disease of cancer to leave my body and my life forever. I strike against it with the awesome healing power of God's light! Where there was once disease there will only be vibrant, healthy tissue. Where was once death there is now a long, healthy, happy life with my family thanks to God's merciful and perfect care.

Within this example we see that blessings can be used to confront or even attack our problems. Directing words of victory towards life's challenges will not only help increase positivity and faith, but it is a chance to strike at the heart of these obstacles with God's matchless healing light. This is also a great opportunity to set some of the terms for your positive outcome and how you believe things will improve on the other side of your crisis. Spoken blessings can help us to take charge, gain control and eventually defeat even life threatening problems, and should be added to any treatment plan to help increase the hope for success.

If you are a Christian then active blessings should always be opened or closed "in the name of Jesus Christ". Including the strength of Christ's promise and mission can be a powerful component within the process of the spoken blessing. Otherwise they can be ended by stating the final word of the blessing or by simply saying amen. In addition to prayer, active blessings can be used to address any issue, problem, addiction or character flaw. So during those low points in life, those slow points, those times when your world is in need of heavenly assistance, speak a blessing. Speak them over your children, your home, your job, your problems and over yourself.

EXERCISE: Blessing your Life with Active Blessings

♦ Now it's your turn to add the power of the spoken blessing to your world. On a separate piece of paper list one or two problems or issues which you would like to improve upon or overcome. Next write a simple active blessing for each. Start learning to speak your blessings when facing these challenges and in moments when you are in need of help or motivation. Over time try to become more inspired in your spoken blessings and practice this process regularly. Have your HP guide help with this exercise.

Everyday Blessings

Everyday blessings are quite different from active blessings but they carry the same life changing power in their own unique fashion. These spoken blessings are not directed at ourselves but are always focused on the wellbeing of those around us. On the surface they may seem like simple encouragements or compliments but when they are delivered by someone who is actively striving to make a better connection with Father, dynamically transformative results can be seen. As God's light increasingly flows through us, simple uplifting conversations with others can carry powerful blessings into their lives. This is a win/win situation for everyone since you are the conduit for God's healing love and spirit when you participate in everyday blessings. So the more people that you bless, the more healing light you yourself are exposed to, and that celestial light will strengthen your soul, heal your body and mind, and will eventually deliver real personal growth and happiness. While everyday blessings can be as simple as a kind word or a friendly smile most often they are impromptu, unscripted phrases of encouragement and loving sentiments of hope. A better understanding of the concept of everyday blessings can be found in the following examples.

Blessing a Friend

Maybe you have a friend that has always been there for you through thick and thin, that loves you unconditionally. The next time that you see them; why not bless them for all of their love and good works? An everyday blessing for such a friend might go something like this:

You are the best friend anyone could ever have. I don't know where I'd be without you. You make the world a better place.

Blessing a Child

Do you have a child? Maybe they're a great kid or perhaps they're troubled and struggle with many of life's challenges. Either way they could probably benefit from some blessings of encouragement from you. The following is just one example of an everyday blessing for a child:

You're a great kid! I know you can do anything that God has planned for you. Be kind to others and do the best you can do, and I know you'll do wonderful things. Remember that I will always love you, no matter what.

Blessing an Acquaintance

Most often when we think about helping others our thoughts naturally travel to family and friends, but what about those that contribute to our wellbeing and happiness on a regular basis but that are not close to us. Perhaps its your favorite cashier at the grocery store, or your mail carrier or the next door neighbor. It could be a coworker or a customer or anyone with whom you make occasional contact, someone that brightens your day from time to time. Well maybe it's time that you brightened theirs? So the next time the school bus driver drops off your child at the bus stop, stick your head in the door and say:

Hey I just wanted to take a second and thank you for the wonderful job you doing. It's always comforting to know someone as great as you is driving my child to school each day. Thanks again for all you do.

Here's an IDEA:

⇒ Turn everyday blessings into a fun game. Each member of your family commits to speaking an everyday blessing over three people they encounter that day. At the dinner table at the end of the day, share your everyday blessing stories with each other and the positive reactions that they inspired. Finally take an informal vote to decide who shared the most inspiring everyday blessing story. This is a game that can be played alone or as a group and is a fun way to get the everyday blessing ball rolling.

Blessing a Stranger

Can you bless people you don't even know? Why not? When you're out and about; why not keep an eye out for new acquaintances that you can bless? It can be something as simple as a someone you encounter who has very well-behaved children. Here is a great chance to bless that person and their children too:

You have some very well-mannered kids there. It's refreshing to see such good kids these days. You've done a great job.

Again to many these will seem like simple compliments but to those that are striving for a greater connection with God they are powerful blessings indeed. How else can you effectively be a conduit for God's spirit if you don't reach out and make some kind of positive connection. And remember that since you are the channel for this healing spiritual light, the more people that you bless equals the more love and healing light that flows into your life. So bless everyone you come in contact with. As God's spirit flows through you, your attitude will improve and your soul will get involved and increase and you will see miracles in your life and the lives of those that you bless.

EXERCISE: Uplifting Others with Everyday Blessings

♦ On a separate piece of paper list at least three people that you can grace with an everyday blessing this week. Once you have blessed them, return to your list and make some notes about the experience, how they reacted and your feelings surrounding it. If you get a chance, bless them again, further reinforcing this exercise. Be sure to share your experiences with your HP guide.

The Spoken Blessing - terms and conditions apply

Spoken blessings have conditions under which they will and will not work. If these terms are not honored, blessings will be limited in their effectiveness.

1) **Both active and everyday blessings** are only effective if the person delivering the blessing is actively striving to make a better connection with God and His plan.

Furthermore **active blessings** will see the most success if the following conditions are honored:

1) You should have prayed about the situation and have received your answer and formulated a plan for success and be earnestly striving to do what you have been asked to do.
2) Keep your motivations pure and inline with the above mentioned plan.
3) Value and care for your current blessings that surround and support the problem you wish to overcome.

Eliminating the Negative Dialogue

If we wish to stay positive and continue to create an environment where the soul can grow in strength and knowledge, then a different approach to positive thinking must be found. An effective way to shift from a pessimistic outlook to one that's more positive and hopeful is to monitor the dialogue in which we regularly participate. In the book of Mark, chapter seven it is recorded that Jesus taught this valuable lesson:

[15] *There is nothing from without a man, that entering into him can defile him: but the things which come out of him, those are they that defile the man.*

Following this passage Jesus gives a laundry list of dark and destructive things that can proceed forth from the hearts of humankind. It can also be said that it is not only the things that come forth from our hearts but from our mouths that defile us as well. If we paid attention, many of us would encounter an endless stream of negativity, gossiping, boastfulness, complaining, and hopelessness coming from our mouths daily. Yes, a habit of these types of utterances will not only defile our souls but they will distance us from God and the lasting happiness that His blessings provide. There is no better way to extinguish the burning fire of faith and belief than to participate in such verbal practices. While you can pray to become more positive in your communications, there is no magic technique for overcoming this problem. The solution is as basic as monitoring our daily dialogue and making corrections to our conversational patterns. While there is no organized exercise in this lesson that assists you in beginning this process, you are encouraged to start monitoring the overall tone of your personal dialogue. Try to begin by making adjustments when you find your conversation drifting into negative, hopeless or generally destructive patterns.

> *" But let him ask in faith, nothing wavering. For he that wavereth is like a wave of the sea driven with the wind and tossed.*
>
> *James 1:6*

Perhaps you have a boss that is hard to deal with and quite often demeaning. You come home every night with the latest tales of how you are being mistreated. You spend the first 30 minutes of most evenings going over and over all of the awful things that happened that day. This leads into revisiting other occurrences from the past that have made you so unhappy. Your displeasure with your boss grows in intensity even bordering on hatred, as you endlessly mull over your seemingly hopeless situation. You may not have noticed it but the once happy demeanor of your family has changed. Your spouse has become visibly uneasy and angry as well, as they begin to rant and rave concerning the injustice of your situation. Your children have become a little more sullen since your arrival as in addition to anger, they begin to feel real fear concerning that fact that someone is mistreating you.

In this example we witness the spirit in a home shifting from one that was happy and peaceful to one that is more dark and foreboding. If God is building a fire escape out of your current situation, participating in such detailed murmuring and hopelessness is smashing that escape route to pieces daily. Instead of drawing God's resolving spirit into your home and life, you are calling in the dark spirit of anger, resentfulness, hopelessness, and despair. This dark spirit has a plan for you alright and that plan involves more of the same. Your boss is carrying a spiritual disease and you and your family have just come down with it, and this sickness if not treated will slow your spiritual progress and possibly take you off the path God has prepared for you.

Of course we all need to confide in someone or vent now and then, but regular participation in faithless, negative conversation will stop us dead in our spiritual tracks. If you find yourself in such a situation it is critical that you search out God's plan for it's resolution and keep trying to stay on that course. Sometimes it takes time to resolve life's problems so stay patient and believe. Watch for improvements and talk about those things at night. On the bad days, try to talk about God's power and love and how He is most likely hard at work trying to create a miracle in your life, and that you just need to give Him time. By doing this you will be maintaining God's spirit in your home and you will then not only be comforted, but you will be able to better hear His guidance and promptings in this and all other situations.

You may have friends or other associates with whom you regularly engage in conversations in which you talk behind peoples backs, or tear them down or complain and gripe about one thing after another. Now is the time to encourage these folks to turn over a new leaf. If you can't help them to stop participating in such backbiting and negativity, it may be time to find a better group of friends. In his letter to the Philippians, the apostle Paul wrote:

....whatsoever things are true, whatsoever things are honest, whatsoever things are just, whatsoever things are pure, whatsoever things are lovely, whatsoever things are of good report; if there be any virtue, and if there be any praise, think on these things.

As people striving for true and lasting happiness for ourselves and others, this should be our motto. These are the types of things that should be coming forth from our mouths, the types of things that are continually attuning us to God's spirit. So begin today monitoring your daily conversations. Practice making adjustments when your dialogue turns negative in any way. If you slip, stop yourself as quickly as you can. Discuss this issue with your spouse and family and enlist their help in shifting the conversation within your home to one that is more uplifting and positive. If people around you start talking negatively, don't reprimand them but instead try to change the subject to something more uplifting. When others are complaining, encourage them and help them find the good within their situation; something for which to be thankful. Be the one to initiate conversations and set the overall tone. Before leaving the house in the morning, find something positive in the news or think of something good that's happening in your community or in your own life that you can bring up in conversation that day that might uplift and inspire others during casual conversations. These techniques not only help others, but they can be invaluable in keeping your own personal environment positive and hopeful. Have your HP guide help you to identify these conversational patterns in your life and to develop a plan to overcome them. If you will do this, you'll be amazed at how quickly and powerfully God's blessings will begin to materialize within your life. You will also begin to feel real peace and hope for yourself, your family and the future.

In this Lesson we have learned:

✓ That the power of the spoken blessing will not only heal and uplift our own souls, but the souls of those around us.

✓ That by shifting our dialogue with others from negative conversational patterns to those that are characterized by love, patience and faith, we will begin to see miracles not only in our own lives but in the lives of those around us.

Making a Commitment

Finally, please commit to memory the following precept concerning positivity and the soul.

MEMORIZE: Personal Precept #6 - Positivity and the Soul

♥ If my soul is to remain healthy and grow, I must speak blessings over the souls of others daily through words of hope, kindness and encouragement.

Forgiveness

- *In this lesson we will develop and reinforce the three concepts of forgiveness within our lives. We will learn to genuinely forgive those in seek of forgiveness and to let go of the pain related to unrepentant offenders. Finally, we will begin developing a habit of forgiving ourselves.*

In Preparation:

- Read teaching eight (pgs. 86-89) of The Happiness Principle.
- Begin focusing on your current feelings about forgiveness and how you deal with those who trespass against you.
- Pray for a better understanding of the true concept of forgiveness and the desire to develop it within your life.

If you have read teaching eight of The Happiness Principle, then you have all of the necessary information to begin on your path to including or improving the gift of forgiveness in your life. And why is forgiveness a gift for you? Because it releases you from the destructive emotions of resentment, anger, frustration, vengeance, and grief that quite often accompany offenses and trespasses. Keep in mind three basic concepts of forgiveness:

1) If someone is sincerely contrite and seeking your forgiveness, then you must try to give it.

2) If the offender does not seek forgiveness then it is not possible to give it. Instead you must now try to let it go and not dwell upon it anymore. Learn from the experience and make adjustments in your life to protect against recurrences of the trespass, but don't continue wrestling with it in your heart. Protect your peace and let it go.

3) Don't forget to include yourself in the process of forgiveness. Life is challenging and we all make mistakes so remember to be kind to yourself and patient with yourself and always try in the end to forgive yourself.

"and be ye kind one to another, tenderhearted, forgiving one another"

Ephesians 4:32

In the following pages we will examine these three aspects of forgiveness as we attempt to begin to incorporate them into our lives.

1) The Obligation of Forgiveness

Some of us flinch at a requirement to forgive. There may be those that have hurt us so badly that the thought of forgiveness is offensive. There is no mandate that says if someone in your life has hurt you in the same fashion over and over again that you must keep taking it till the end of time. The mandate is that we must try to be empathetic and understanding if it is a problem with which they are struggling and seemingly trying to overcome. This is the most challenging part of forgiveness. If a close friend speaks some unkind words and then later comes back and apologizes, and then never does anything like it again, forgiveness is a simple and easy process. It is the repeat offenders that can pose the greatest challenge. We must bear in mind that as we try to improve and grow, we will need the patience, love and understanding of those around us, so if we want to be forgiven we must try to forgive.

But what if your husband has cheated on you in the past, not just once but more than once? You have struggled through the painful process of reconciliation and forgiveness but you find one day that he's back at it again. He comes to you once more, remorsefully begging your forgiveness, claiming that he doesn't know why he keeps doing these things over and over again. Does the obligation of forgiveness demand that you pardon him and try anew one more time? Not necessarily. While eventual forgiveness in some form is required, it is up to you, whether or not you want to get off of this life draining merry-go-round. Actually staying in the marriage might make it almost impossible to genuinely forgive at this point.

If you decide to end the marriage, this might eventually put you in a position where you can realize that your husband is a troubled man with a serious problem. While you were hurt terribly, soon you may be in a place where you can have a little empathy toward him and his pathetic situation and while you are finished going back for more, you should start trying to let it go. All of this said, if you stay or if you go, eventually forgiveness must be a part of the agenda if the individual is *sincerely* seeking it. Now some offenses are great and forgiveness may take time, but we must try to eventually grant this type of forgiveness in one form or another. While there is no organized exercise in connection with the first concept of forgiveness, you are encouraged to ponder and pray upon any offenses in the past in which you were unwilling to forgive when forgiveness has been *sincerely* proffered. If there is any way you can release yourself and that person from this burden please do. While you're at it; have you committed any trespasses for which you have not made amends? Pray about them and if you feel so inspired, make them right.

2) Letting It Go

So what if the offender doesn't want your forgiveness? Perhaps they feel they have done nothing wrong or they know that they have hurt you but they just don't care, or perhaps they are happy that they have hurt you and would do it again if given the chance. If there are unrepentant people in your life that are seriously hurting you on a regular basis and just don't care, some of the responsibility is on you. So if the unrepentant offender has hurt you greatly or is great at hurting you, you have some choices to make. If you continue your association with these unapologetic people, *letting it go* will be almost impossible because you can be assured that more abuse is on the way. If you can modify your exposure to these people in the future and minimize opportunities for a recurrence of such trespasses then the process of *letting it go* can begin. Now some offenses are greater than others so pray about this process and try to do it in the right time and fashion. The whole point is to find a place in your life where you no longer dwell upon these offenses and you have gained a level of personal peace concerning them.

Here's an IDEA:

⇒ One of the easiest ways to avoid the trying process of forgiveness is to strive to never take offense too easily. Try not to read too much into what others are saying or doing. Even if their intentions are less than honorable, take care not to react or overreact too quickly. Keep your cool and laugh it off later in a quiet moment. If the offender unremorsefully continues to repeat such trespasses during future encounters, look beyond the emotional prompting to retaliate and you will probably hear a better prompting from your Father in Heaven that will guide you to distance yourself from this unrepentant person and future destructive interactions.

One of the key aspects of the concept of *letting it go* is making a commitment to try not to think upon or talk about the offense again. Nursing an old grudge is like feeding a cancer that continues to eat away at you and destroy you. So if you want to let it go, the cycle of regret and recrimination must end. This does not mean that you must let down your guard and allow the person back in to use and abuse you once more, but it does mean that when the battle is over, we must put down our weapons and try never to pick them up again. If the incident arises in your mind, go find something uplifting to do. Think on things that are positive and hopeful, and of course pray. Pray for God's peace concerning the matter and the ability to let it go once and for all. If friends and family bring the issue back up again, be prepared with the following statement, "I need to put it behind me now so I'm trying not to talk about it anymore." Be respectful since these folks will most likely believe they are revisiting the offense in support of you, but it's very important that they are helped to understand that you can't go back to that dark place anymore.

In the following exercise you will be asked to recall great trespasses made against you that periodically resurface in memory or discussion. Please be careful not to revisit offenses which you haven't thought about for years and years; those about which you have already found peace. Don't use this exercises to reopen wounds that have already healed. Instead pray for discernment to indentify things that still come up in your heart and mind periodically; issues that you just can't seem to get past. Once you have identified the offenses, you should outline how often thoughts of the offenses arise in your heart and mind and the emotions that accompany them. Next build a plan to overcome the destructive cycle of emotions that relate to the offense. Finally, get to work applying the plan and putting these issues away once and for all. So let's say for the sake of illustration that your brother's ex-wife is a gossip and she still associates with much of your family and a few of your friends. In the past she has spread a lot of hurtful and untrue rumors about you and your husband. Another close family member feels that it is their duty to keep you informed of everything this person is saying behind your back. While you have distanced yourself from this woman and you cut short or avoid family gatherings which she attends, her slanderous deeds continue to haunt you. The following example illustrates how you might utilize the upcoming exercise to approach such an issue:

THE PROBLEM WITH GOSSIPING JANE

OFFENSE: MY EX-SISTER-IN-LAW JANE AND HER DESTRUCTIVE GOSSIPING.

MY FEELINGS: SOME OF THE RUMORS SHE HAS SPREAD ARE JUST TERRIBLE AND I'M AFRAID OTHERS ARE BELIEVING HER. I WORRY IF OTHERS ARE TALKING BEHIND MY BACK TOO. I THINK ABOUT IT MANY TIMES A WEEK. THE WHOLE MESS EATS ME UP.

MY PLAN: I WILL REMIND MYSELF THAT SINCE SHE ALSO SPREADS RUMORS ABOUT OTHERS, I AM NOT THE PROBLEM BUT SHE IS. SHE IS A SAD, NEGATIVE, DESTRUCTIVE PERSON. I WILL ASK MY FAMILY TO STOP GIVING ME UPDATES CONCERNING HER LATEST SLANDERS. I WILL PRAY TO NO LONGER DWELL ON HER LIES AND FOR ASSISTANCE IN ELIMINATING FUTURE CONTACT WITH HER.

EXERCISE: Letting Go of Past Offenses

♦ On a separate piece of paper list one or two past offenses that still haunt you today. Next discuss the frequency in which the issues arises in your mind and the related emotions that you experience. Now formulate a plan for permanently letting go of the offenses and the poisonous emotions that accompany them. Make sure that prayer is part of the plan. Finally, apply the plan. Have your HP Guide help you develop and apply a plan that in time will eliminate such toxic trespasses from your conversation, your memory and your life.

Going The Extra Mile

So now that you've let it go; could you take it a step further? Could you now pray for the unrepentant trespasser? Could you speak a blessing for them? Seem crazy? Well that's just what Jesus encouraged us to do in the fifth chapter of Matthew, when He said:

[44]*But I say unto you, Love your enemies, bless them that curse you, do good to them that hate you, and pray for them which despitefully use you, and persecute you;* [45]*that ye may be the children of your Father which is in heaven:*

So why would we be asked to pray for or speak blessings over those that desire to hurt us or even destroy us? While such an act might seem on its surface to be selfless, if we look a little deeper we find some powerful personal benefits.

1st - If our enemy's attitude improves then our lives and the lives of others benefit. As Jesus directs, by using the power of prayer and the spoken blessing, the heart of the unrepentant offender can be softened and their manner and focus can be changed for the better. An ex-husband who has done horrible things in the past could become a better father and example to your kids. A difficult coworker might become more tolerable and this would not just help you but it could improve the work environment for everyone. If you can't bring yourself to *love* them, consider *empathizing* with their sad and destructive state and pray for a spiritual healing of sorts on their behalf. It may be one of the hardest things you'll ever do, but if you'll utilize the power of prayer and blessings on behalf of your enemies, you might just help turn a tiger into a pussycat.

2nd - When someone attacks us, the common response that rises within most is to attack back. If someone acts hateful toward us, we can tend to react in an hateful manner. It's as if the attacker is infected with an highly contagious virus. In an instant a person who is peaceful by nature can become angry and vindictive, while a happy person can find themselves fearful and even depressed. But if we apply this wonderful principle found within the concept of forgiveness, it becomes impossible to be vengeful when you are blessing your enemy and you are less likely to feel down when you are praying over the situation. In effect, you have just been immunized from the destructive spiritual disease that accompanies such people.

3rd - Finally, we have been promised that by way of this process, we will become children of our Heavenly Father. In other words we will become *favored* children of God. A favored child has a closer relationship and receives preferential treatment. Since the goal of The Happiness Principle is to achieve a better connection with God then this just might be a powerful path to accomplishing that purpose and receiving a greater fullness of his blessings.

3) Forgiving Yourself

Some of us live in a state of regret and self-incrimination for large portions of our lives. Even when we have made amends for past mistakes, they can oftentimes resurface to haunt us like a ghost from the past. If we dwell on the past or are overly self-critical we must learn to apply this last concept of forgiveness. This stage of forgiveness is not just about resolving past missteps but it can also be used to help eliminate character flaws and destructive tendencies with which we may have wrestled for years.

Personal Statements of Self-Forgiveness

Forgiveness is a precious gift and it must first be offered before it can be received. It's helpful to formally offer a *statement of self-forgiveness* for any past issue or mistake for which you have repented, overcome and made amends but that continues to resurface in your heart and mind.

So if you were not there for your children the first few years of their lives but you have now corrected that situation and made amends and nagging regrets continue to surface, a personal statement of self-forgiveness might go something like this:

I forgive myself for not being there for my kids. We are now together and stronger than ever, so I will not let the past spoil this blessing.

This type of statement can be repeated when regrets of resolved mistakes from the past arise. Try to keep them simple and to the point. They are basic reminders of why you no longer need to "go there" anymore. These statements can also be used to assist in overcoming destructive personal patterns. So say that you have a habit of comparing yourself to others. You have a great life and many blessings but you often struggle to be happy because some of your friends and neighbors are doing better than you in certain ways. You can begin to overcome this personal attack upon your talents and your many blessings with a statement of forgiveness:

I forgive myself for making personal comparisons with others. I am thankful and happy about my individual talents and blessings. I am valuable in the eyes of my family and my God and I don't need validation from anyone else.

If you find yourself in the midst of regret, negative self-talk or thoughts that diminish your self-worth and your connection to God, use personal statements of forgiveness to identify and dismiss these dark motivators. They are simple and basic so there's no need to script them; just let them come. Actively forgive yourself on a regular basis and dismiss the dark approaches that would keep you mired in negativity and in past mistakes, and embrace the hopeful future that God has waiting for you. Have your HP Guide help you in your quest for self-forgiveness.

In this Lesson we have learned:

✓ That we *must* try to forgive those that truthfully seek forgiveness, if we expect to be forgiven for our trespasses. If the offender is not repentant then we *must* work to let it go in an appropriate fashion.

✓ If we have earnestly tried to make restitution and repent of wrongs we have committed in the past, then we *must* start forgiving ourselves. Finally, we should forgive ourselves for destructive personal thought patterns and habits as a powerful reminder that they have no place in a happy and blessed future.

Making a Commitment

Finally, please commit to memory the following precept concerning forgiveness.

MEMORIZE: Personal Precept #7 - Forgiveness

♥ I will learn to give the gift of forgiveness to myself and to those in my life who truly seek it. Otherwise I will learn from the experience and try to let it go.

The Power of Love

- *In this lesson we will learn about the nature of pure love and charity and its place in our lives. Next we will learn how to draw more of this powerful light not only into our own lives but into the lives of others.*

In Preparation:

- Read teaching eleven (pgs. 106 -117) of The Happiness Principle.
- Begin focusing on the current state of love in your life. Love of family, love of friends and love of God.
- Pray for a better understanding of the concept of pure love and charity.

In The Happiness Principle we read that pure love and charity go hand in hand, and that this form of love is a powerful spirit or energy, and that this Celestial light is the greatest power in the Universe.

In the first epistle of John, the apostle writes expressly concerning the very nature of God:

7 Beloved, let us love one another: for love is of God; and every one that loveth is born of God, and knoweth God.

8 He that loveth not knoweth not God; for God is love.

In this passage John makes it clear that "God is love." In other words, God is a powerful being of light and the energy or matter that constitutes this ultimate eternal being is the light of pure love. He also teaches us that if we wish to know God then we too must always strive to attune to this light of love. The Happiness Principle teaches that we cannot be happy in a true and lasting fashion if we don't make a clear and functioning connection with God, so the pure light of charitable love must be at the top of our list of personal priorities. But how do you begin to attain this premiere virtue or improve upon the charitable attitude that you've already acquired? Well first it is helpful to do a quick analysis of your daily life and search for areas in which you're lacking in the department of love and charity. While we could list all of the ways that you are succeeding in this regard and provide praise for all of your good works, that wouldn't really help identify those places and attitudes where love does not exist and improvements can be made.

> *"And now abideth faith, hope, charity, these three; but the greatest of these is charity."*
>
> *1 Corinthians 13:13*

Where is the Love?

As you look at your average day, do you see from yourself actions and attitudes that inspire pure love from others? Perhaps you're not feeling a lot of love toward other people. Maybe most of them just don't seem very lovable. Do you feel the desire to be helpful to others and if so, how often do you act upon that desire? Are there moments of anger, contention or even yelling during an average day and how do you think that is effecting the light of pure love in your life? If we want to get in tune with the energy of love then our actions must begin to match the frequency of this divine healing light. At the least we must begin to resist actions and reactions that tune us away from this all important connection. We can accomplish this in a gradual fashion through what are known as *acts of love*. It is through these simple daily works that we can establish and maintain the flow of pure love into our lives.

Acts of Love

The term *acts of love* might inspire thoughts of great and lavish deeds but in reality true acts of love are simple yet powerful daily actions that will not only help draw us closer to God, but will also help others improve upon their own divine connection. Again the use of a few basic examples to illustrate the concept of *acts of love* might be useful here:

Lending a Hand

As we travel along life's path are we willing to lend a hand when help is needed from those around us? If we have the time and are able, do we act to lend loving support even to those we do not know? If you are in the grocery store parking lot and someone politely approaches you because they have a dead car battery and need a jump; how do you respond? You have jumper cables in the trunk and you are not in a rush nor do you have anything scheduled in the immediate future. Is your first impression, "Hey I want to help this person because I know how stressful and frustrating it can be to have your car breakdown and to be in need of assistance." Or is your response more along the lines of, "Wow, what an inconvenience. I need to tell this person that I don't have cables and get out of here as quick as possible." If it seems like a safe situation and you have the time, the loving thing to do is to invest a little of that time into helping someone out. Imagine what our world would be like if everyone had such a loving, charitable attitude. So powerful acts of love can be as simple as helping an elderly person get their groceries into their car, or giving a neighbor a hand steadying the ladder as they clean leaves out of their rain gutters, or stopping and visiting at the home of an acquaintance that you know is struggling in life, rather than hurriedly passing them by. It's the little things that not only produce a blanket of love throughout our neighborhoods and communities, but they are regular exercises that strengthen the spirit of pure love in our own lives. Please remember to resist becoming overwhelmed by this process, believing that every issue and problem in your world and the world at large is your responsibility to fix. Learn to become inspired in your charity. We need to learn when it's time to help and the extent to which we should go in that service. Remember that you are not here to save the whole world but to care for your own corner of it. If everyone was able to identify and fulfill their own individual God given calling, the world's problems would vanish quite quickly, and real love and of course happiness would be our common creed.

> *"My little children, let us not love in word, neither in tongue; but in deed and in truth."*
>
> *1 John 3:18*

Saying Sorry

It's hard to say you're sorry even when you know that you're wrong but what about when you think you're right? What about when you KNOW you're right? Could you ever apologize in order to protect the spirit of peace and love in your home? One of the most powerful acts of love is being willing to diffuse a contentious situation in order to protect God's loving spirit in your life and the lives of others. So the next time you're in a argument with your spouse, could you perhaps take a moment and take a breath and make the choice to make a sacrifice and stop the destructive spirit of conflict in your home? At the least, could you apologize for participating in such contention and for speaking to them in such a disrespectful fashion? Perhaps the next time things get a little tense or heated with a coworker, rather than letting it run it's course, why not go to them later, once things have calmed down a little, and make peace. Find some common ground and tell them that you're sorry. If you will learn to treat people in this manner, you will find that many of them will drop their guard, open up and will begin to treat you with greater respect and love. So be the bigger person and do the right thing... the loving thing.

Charitable Giving

As they sat in view of the church treasury, Jesus and His disciples watched as many people even those of great wealth made sizeable donations to the church. As a woman approached and placed two small coins into the donation receptacle, Jesus called His disciple's attention to a powerful concept. In the book of Luke, chapter 12 He explains:

[43] *And he called unto him his disciples, and saith unto them, Verily I say unto you, That this poor widow hath cast more in, than all they which have cast into the treasury:*

[44] *For all they did cast in of their abundance; but she of her want did cast in all that she had, even all her living.*

In this passage Jesus points out that there is power in giving, especially when that sacrifice is made in a place of need or want, and it is a wonderful act of love. Whenever we give part of our income in a charitable fashion it is a wonderful thing, but the real test is if we can continue to have faith and charity in our hearts when we find ourselves lacking. So if your having a rough year financially and your concerned that your not going to have much of a Christmas, could you still throw a few dollars in the donation kettle outside your local store during the holidays? Could you buy a toy for very needy children, even if your kids are not going to have the greatest holiday season ever? Could you donate some food to the hungry, even when you're worried about how you're going to pay some of the bills next month? You see a charitable heart is not one that gives conditionally, but it is the heart that is kind and giving at all times and it is that heart that attunes the best to God's loving spirit. The true charitable heart is smart and inspired in it's giving. So if you are moved upon by God's spirit to give, give generously and in time you will not only be blessed with abundance but you will also be blessed with more of God's Celestial light of pure love.

Giving Credit to Others

We all love being right. It's not uncommon to have the desire to always be the one with "the answer". What if we allowed the other guy to have the answer now and then? Wouldn't it be an amazing act of love to encourage others to develop their confidence and ability in the areas of communication and problem solving? In this ever increasingly competitive world it's easy to get caught up in the desire to constantly debate and contradict others, but what if we gave our own egos a break and allowed someone else to shine? If we must constantly proclaim the phrase "I know" when in conversation, we're actually short changing ourselves because when we shut down others to satisfy our own pride, we are missing out on a wealth of information and wisdom that might have come forth from that person. So periodically step out of the way and let someone else have center stage. It's truly a caring act of love.

Here's an IDEA:

⇒ Start teaching others the true meaning of love. You can do this with family, or during a break with coworkers or even on a bus with a stranger. Mention that you're working on a lesson in a self-improvement workbook and that you're interested in the opinions of others. Ask them to express their views on "what love is to them" and then take the opportunity to share what you have learned about love by way of The Happiness Principle and inspire more love in your life and the lives of others.

Making Room for More Love

Are there areas in your life that could use more love? Perhaps there are behavior patterns that eat away at the peace and love that you already have. Is there someone you know that has been struggling and could use a hand? Now is the time to identify these issues and address them with acts of love. While eventually the process that produces these acts will become more natural for you, the following exercise will begin to encourage you to find troubled areas in your life and the lives of others that might be healed with acts of love. First list the issue or recurring problem. Then write down a brief description of the issue and how it is negatively effecting your peace and the light of love in your life. Next describe an act of love that might assist in eliminating this issue from your life and that might restore the spirit of love in your heart. Finally, get to work applying your healing act of love. The following example should provide a basic understanding of how this exercise is conducted. So for the sake of this example let's say that you have a turbulent relationship with your sister. Growing up the two of you fought like cats and dogs and your parents didn't really do much to teach you otherwise. Now that you're both adults you get along better but you still contend with one another on a regular basis and some of this contention can at times get quite heated and personal. Many of these exchanges leave you feeling angry, vindictive and extremely frustrated as you can dwell on these encounters for weeks. You realize that these interactions are negatively effecting your personal peace and attuning you away from God's spirit of pure love. So now that you have identified the problem, you decide that the appropriate act of love is to approach your sister in a peaceful moment and offer a permanent truce. You tell her that you have learned that these fights are hurting not only your relationship but your collective personal peace and most damaging is that it is blocking the love that should exist between two close family members. So you both agree to avoid the usual topics that predictably start these fights. You also agree to try to bite your lip and walk away when signs of coming contentions are seen. Finally, you agree to try to talk positively about one another in casual conversation when you are apart or you won't speak of each other at all. The following is an example of how such a plan might be detailed in the next exercise:

Acts of Love
Issue = Fighting with my sister

Details: My sister and I have really big fights at least once or twice a month. We are very competitive and sometimes fight over things that don't matter just to be right. While I love her, sometimes I actually resent her and treat her like a hated enemy. We tear each other down when talking to other people and sometimes draw other family members into our fights. We have fought all of our lives but now the hard feelings are beginning to run deep and some of the things that are being said are getting to be really over the top. Most of the time we get along and when we are getting along our relationship is fun and fulfilling so I want to try to save the relationship.

Act of Love: I'm going to sit down with my sister and see if she would be willing to talk about the fighting, not the details of the fights, but the effect of the fighting itself. I will see if she's willing to agree to disagree and start working on avoiding and diffusing future fights in order to protect our love for each other and heal the wounds we have created. I'm hoping we can agree to hold our tongues when future contention begins to develop and just walk away. We should agree to always speak kindly to and about each other, and I'll ask her to pray with me for our success.

EXERCISE: Acts of Love

♦ Discover areas in your life or the lives of those around you that are in need of an act of love. On a separate piece of paper list two or three of these issues. Detail each problem and then list an act of love that will overcome each issue. Finally get to work making your acts of love a reality. In addition to this exercise, be sure to look for unplanned opportunities to participate in acts of love throughout each day. Have your HP guide help you with this exercise.

The Greatest Love of All

In the book *The Happiness Principle* we learn that the greatest love of all is the love that we have for God. It is the embodiment of the principle in that we must make God our highest priority if we wish to find true happiness and fulfillment, so loving God is a big part of this equation. In fact we are promised that if we will develop a close, loving relationship with Him, we will be blessed in great and unimaginable ways. In the second chapter of first Corinthians, the Apostle Paul makes an amazing promise:

[9] *But it is written, Eye hath not seen, nor ear heard, neither have entered into the heart of man, the things which God hath prepared for them that love him.*

So by truly loving God we are literally opening the doors to great blessings even blessings that have not been previously experienced, and to unlimited possibilities for peace and contentment. We can begin by always expressing our love for God in prayer, and by asking for divine help and a true desire in making this connection. Of course love is more than just words. It is our actions and attitudes that really demonstrate our love for God. In order to really love someone deeply and completely, we must be true to them. If they are worth loving then we should be consistently committed to them through the good times and the bad. So when times get tough do we blame God? When faced with great difficulty do we participate in behaviors that are rebellious and destructive in spite of Him? Do we lose faith in Him when things aren't going our way? Conversely, do we ignore Him when things are going well and only talk to Him when we are in need? If we treated a spouse or a family member in this fashion, not only would they not feel loved, but our relationship with them would be on shaky ground. So don't be a fair-weather friend when it comes to your relationship with God, but instead love Him consistently and completely through the good and the bad and you will be blessed with the greatest power for healing and happiness in the universe.

In this Lesson we have learned:

✓ That love is more than just an emotion but that it is a Celestial light that can transform our lives and the lives of those around us, and that we can tap into this pure energy by including powerful acts of love within our daily life.

✓ That the greatest love of all is found in the personal relationship that we build with God, and that in order to develop and protect that relationship, we must be consistently dedicated to Him in the good times and the bad.

Making a Commitment

Finally, please commit to memory the following precept concerning the power of love.

> **MEMORIZE: Personal Precept #8 - The Power of Love**
>
> ♥ I will learn to cultivate God's pure love in my own life and the lives of others through daily acts of love, while making a personal and loving relationship with God my highest priority.

Becoming a Person of Integrity

- *In this lesson we will learn about the concept of integrity of character and how it can help us make a more fine tuned connection with God and His love and blessings.*

In Preparation:

- There is no reading assignment with this lesson.
- Begin focusing on your current opinions about "integrity of character" and the state of this concept in your life.
- Pray for a greater understanding of true integrity and for a desire to gain more of it in your life.

A basic definition of the concept of *integrity of character* is as follows:

The quality of being honest and having strong moral principles, and consistently being true to those principles.

This concept is so multifaceted that a basic definition just doesn't do it justice. Perhaps a better way to understand integrity is to examine other words that are synonymous with it. The following are just a few synonyms of integrity:

Honesty, probity, rectitude, honor, good character, principled, ethical, moral, righteousness, virtuous, decency, fairness, scrupulousness, sincerity, truthfulness, trustworthiness.

As you can see, when we look at the synonyms of integrity a powerful concept emerges. God's character consists of all of these wonderful qualities and many more. In the physical world at some point, most children feel the innate desire to be like their earthly parents especially parents that are loving, reliable and consistent. If this trend continues, over time they will adopt similar character traits to those of their parents. In time this will make it easier for these children to receive future guidance and blessings from their parents, and these positive character traits will follow and support them throughout adulthood.

> *"The just man walketh in his integrity: his children are blessed after him."*
>
> *Proverbs 20:7*

This model carries over into the spiritual realm where God is concerned. Again, God is a being of perfect character and integrity and if we further wish to connect with Him and successfully do His works here upon the earth, we too must strive for integrity of character. Now developing such a trait is certainly a long term proposition but if we will get to work today building this powerful quality, in time we will have a spiritual guarantee of lasting balance, blessings and bliss. Of equal importance will be the wonderful example that we will be setting for our children, family and friends to follow.

Roadblocks to Integrity

While the most obvious obstacles to the development of integrity are bad habits, uncontrolled impulses, and misplaced priorities, one of the largest roadblocks is past mistakes. The thought of our past mistakes and weaknesses can cause us to feel unworthy of becoming people of standards today. After all if you participated in such poor behaviors in the past, you have less moral authority to live as a person of standards in the present. Don't fall for this lie. If you have identified your past actions as destructive and turned away from them, you are actually in a unique position to not only help yourself but to help others. You've gone through it and you have a story to tell. You are not a hypocrite but a person that is prevailing over toxic habits and actions, and you carry a valuable testimony that might just help others avoid such damaging pitfalls. You are striving to be a respectful child of God and you are awakening and growing in the light of His pure love. So don't let such falsehoods slow you on your quest for a greater connection with Him through development of personal integrity.

The Golden Rule of Integrity

In the book of Luke chapter six, Jesus shares a foundational concept that can be used to develop more integrity of character.

" Lead your life so you wouldn't be ashamed to sell the family parrot to the town gossip."

Will Rogers

[31]And as ye would that men should do to you, do ye also to them likewise.

Over the years the underlying principle in this passage has become better known as *The Golden Rule*:

Do unto others as you would have them do unto you.

This famous teaching encourages us to treat people the way we would like to be treated. If we try every day to live by this one simple rule, over time integrity of character will follow. By *honestly* applying The Golden Rule you will instantly know what a person of integrity would do in every situation. So let's dive right in with an example of how this works.

So for the sake of this example let's say that you are out for a walk in your neighborhood on a beautiful, crisp fall day. You have been struggling with financial troubles this year and you've found that these walks really help alleviate the stress. As you stroll along in admiration of the beautiful colors in the changing leaves, you notice something on the sidewalk just ahead of you. When you reach it, you realize it's a wallet. As you stoop down to pick it up, you find that it's made of fine leather, not that $9.95 imitation stuff. Inside you find credit cards, family photos and an ID indicating that it belongs to someone who lives just a few miles away from you. You are familiar with this man's neighborhood since it is one of the most affluent areas in your town, as only some of the most wealthy can afford to live there. Finally you shift your attention to the bill fold section of the wallet, where you discover over $400.00 in cash. A rush of adrenaline races through your body as you realize the value of your find. Your first thought is that this is an answer to your prayers and with the holidays coming, your head will be above the financial waters for the first time in months. Next a chain of justifications bear down on you like a roaring freight train. "This guy has lots of money. He will never miss it." you reason. You try to convince yourself that this is God's way of miraculously blessing you; a 'taking from the haves and giving to the have-nots' kind of thing.

Now in this same situation the spirit of The Golden Rule is encouraging you to take a different approach. It asks you to consider, free of rationalization, how you would feel if you lost your wallet. What would you desire of someone that found your lost wallet? This answer is quite simple. We all would hope that our wallet was found by an honest person that would make it a priority to return it and all of it's contents. There can be no rationalizing when applying this principle since rationalizations tarnish The Golden Rule. If you find yourself rationalizing that if you were a wealthy person and lost your wallet, you would want the needy person who found it to keep the money, you are attempting to bend the Golden Rule to suit your own purposes. In fact a certain amount of common sense and a whole lot of honesty is required to effectively utilize The Golden Rule in pursuit of greater integrity of character. In this example The Golden Rule teaches us that a person of integrity is an honest person that would return the wallet and it's contents no matter the circumstances. If we will try to consistently demonstrate integrity in every area of our lives, God will help us resolve many of life's problems in a lasting and honest fashion, and that includes financial issues. The Golden Rule teaches us that since we wish to be treated with kindness, we should be kind to others. It encourages us to be respectful of others if we wish to be respected and asks us to be patient if we want others to show patience towards us. The Golden Rule encourages us toward generosity, forgiveness, compassion, honesty, values, morality, virtue, decency, sincerity, truthfulness, trustworthiness, politeness, friendliness, cleanliness, courteousness, gratitude, and mercy just to name a few. Once again all of these virtues are synonymous with integrity, so let the Golden Rule be your guide to ever growing integrity of character.

A Person of Growing Integrity

There is no such thing as a person of "perfect integrity". Nobody's perfect and we all face challenges concerning our character. Integrity of character is not a road that's traveled with an ultimate destination but it is a journey that will last for the rest of our lives. Like caring for a house plant, we never reach a point where we no longer need to provide it nourishment and care. Likewise if we make it a priority to care for our ever growing personal integrity, in time it will bloom into a life changing, life saving force and will be a blessing to everyone around us. So remember that you don't have to be perfect to be a person of integrity but you must be someone who is consistently trying to make it's development a priority in your life. In the beginning it might be helpful to consider yourself a person of growing integrity; a person that makes mistakes but that is determined to keep trying.

The Golden Ruler

The following exercise is called *The Golden Ruler* and based on the principle of The Golden Rule it can help us identify and begin to transform areas in our lives and places in our hearts that are in need of integrity of character. We are all familiar with rulers. A ruler is a measuring stick that is used for measurements and to make straight lines. The Golden Ruler can be used much like a standard ruler to measure those personal areas that may be in need of improvement and to keep our paths through life straight. When you look at a standard ruler, you will see markings that reflect inches and centimeters. Imagine The Golden Ruler as having markings such as honesty, morality, gratitude and compassion, markings that measure the qualities of integrity that The Golden Rule reveals. By holding The Golden Ruler up to certain areas of our lives, a need for improvement is quite often instantly revealed.

Here's an IDEA:

⇒ Here's a way to find areas of your life that could gain greater integrity by using The Golden Ruler exercise. Simply collect a few of the synonyms of integrity that were mentioned earlier in this lesson. Next look up each word in the dictionary, regardless of whether or not you believe you already understand their meaning. Finally, ponder on how you are doing with each concept in your own life and make a note of areas that could use some improvement.

This exercise is a long term proposition meaning that you don't just work on it for a week or two and then move on. You are asked to work on one main issue through The Golden Ruler exercise until you return the next time to this point in the lesson manual in the future. Whether it be six weeks or six months or a year, you will continue to place a special focus on improving this single aspect of your character until you return to this lesson and apply The Golden Ruler to another major area of your life. The following examples will help demonstrate how The Golden Ruler exercise can be applied to achieve increased integrity of character:

Your Cheating Heart

This example supposes that overall and outwardly, you are an honest person. You are well respected by those that know you and if asked, most of your friends and neighbors would describe you as a trustworthy and reliable person. What most don't know is that in the little unseen areas of your world you live a different lifestyle. A short list of some of your unnoticed activities are as follows. A couple of years ago, you had a friend hook-up illegal cable TV at your home and ever since you've been receiving free entertainment, saving hundreds and hundreds of dollars. At your job you

> *" Integrity is doing the right thing, even when no one is watching."*
>
> *C.S. Lewis*

show up late when you know your supervisor won't be there and leave a little early whenever you get the chance. While at work you just do the bare minimum, pacing yourself most of the day, avoiding additional responsibilities whenever possible. At the grocery store when the cashier gives you too much change, you instinctively pocket it without a thought of pointing out the error. Yes, outwardly you are a good person. You appear kind and even caring to others but you have a hidden life that needs some work.

When you hold The Golden Ruler up to this side of your character, the flaws are instantly revealed. The Golden Rule asks that you pay for your cable. After all if you had a business; how would you feel if others were stealing from you? Where your employer is concerned, they are giving you a wage that you agreed upon when you were hired. A wage that is being exchanged for certain amount of effort on your part. The Golden Rule encourages you to live up to your end of the bargain and give an honest days work for an honest days pay. The Golden Rule has something to say about the cashier at the market as well. It wants you to consider that she is most likely going to have to pay for the mistake she made when you received too much change. That's right it's coming out of her pocket at the end of the day. The Golden Rule encourages you to correct such mistakes immediately because if you take the extra money knowingly, you are participating in theft, pure and simple. By using The Golden Ruler in this instance you identify that you are struggling in the area of honesty in your life. It's time to make a commitment to try to be true and forthright in every area of your life, especially the unseen ones. Turn over a new leaf, make amends, and make a change. Disconnect the cable and start paying for it or learn to live without it. Make a new commitment to your employer and start giving it your best. You will not only be helping your company by living up to your responsibilities but your family will benefit through the job recognition, advancements and wage increases that should follow in time. Be true not only to your friends and family but to strangers like the girl at the check stand by pointing out errors such as too much change. You will be amazed at the response that you get. It's an unfortunate commentary on the world in which we live, how shocked and thankful people act at such a gesture. Look for any other areas of your life where honesty is an issue and keep after them. By using The Golden Ruler exercise to identify these types of character flaws, and then by making a commitment to make a change, greater integrity will follow.

Devaluing Virtue

While the next example operates from a man's perspective, the ladies should be able to appreciate and even gain from this one as well. This example presupposes that you are a man in your mid-thirty's. You have been in multiple live-in relationships over the years and one unsuccessful marriage. Since then you've come to the conclusion that these romantic associations are more trouble than they're worth. In your mind the only positive that has come from these relationships is your beautiful five year old daughter. With all of the arguing and fighting for control, you've decided that the only commitment you're going to be making in the future is one of long term bachelorhood.

All of this said, you haven't given up on the ladies completely. Quite often on the weekends, you get together with a few of your closest friends and head out to the clubs and the bars for some fun. The main goals: To drink, party and hookup with women. Now when we use the term "hookup" here, we are not using it in the traditional sense of simply meeting up but in the more current meaning of this slang term, namely to have sex. Sometimes you hookup with women that you've hooked up with before and some of these connections last for more than one night, perhaps a week or two or three but they always come to an end for one reason or

> *"Always do right. This will gratify some people and astonish the rest."*
>
> *Mark Twain*

another. Your favorite part of this process is meeting new women you've never been with before and eventually hooking up with them. Again you have no intention of making a long term connection, let alone a commitment with any one of these ladies. Sure you enjoy the companionship at times, but in reality you are interested in one thing - the hookup. The few times you've had to defend this behavior in the past, you've used the standard justifications like "Consenting adults" and "I didn't make any promises." and "Nobody held a gun to her head."

Now if you have the courage to hold The Golden Ruler up to this part of your life, you might just find a few problems. You may not have the ability to think like a woman but if you did, you'd find that most do not think like you. Most, no matter how sexually active, in the end are hoping for a long term commitment and to live happily ever after. If you have a mother or a sister, The Golden Rule encourages you to realize that in no way would you want others to use these special people in your life, the way you are using the random women in yours. What about your five year old daughter? What are your greatest hopes and dreams for her when she grows up? Is it to be lost and searching for a relationship, all the while being passed around by strange men until she finds one? How about the increasingly antiquated concept of being a gentleman? Gentlemen respect woman, they don't take advantage of them and they honor them rather than use them. A true man of integrity is always a gentleman. If you've struggled to find a lasting relationship with that one special girl, it's probably because you've neglect to first build the most important relationship of all; your relationship with your Heavenly Father. Dating and marriage are some of the most important things in which you will ever participate, and they require great inspiration and guidance from God if you're to be successful. Before you will find your Miss Right, God probably needs to turn you into somebody's Mr. Right. And this applies to the ladies out there also. Require more from the men that you date. Help them be gentlemen and teach them to honor you and your virtue. If they won't; then you know that being a man of integrity is not a priority to them and they're probably not going to provide long term happiness. Teach your children the concepts of chastity and virtue. Raise them with a strong connection to God and reassure them that He will then help them find someone who will love and honor them forever. Integrity is not complete without moral character.

The List Goes On and On

It doesn't have to be just honesty or virtue but any area of your life in which The Golden Ruler reveals a need for improvement.

EXERCISE: The Golden Ruler

♦ Hold The Golden Ruler up to a few of the areas of your life and when you find one that doesn't measure up, it's time to get to work. List the offending character trait on a piece of paper and then write down some instances and details of this tendency. Next list a few ways in which you might begin to turn this weakness into a strength. Finally, get to work applying your plan. Make restitution, make amends and make the changes necessary to begin to gain greater integrity of character in this area of your life. Work on this issue until you return to this lesson in the future. When you do, write down a few thoughts on your progress in this area. Have your HP Guide help you with this exercise.

Integrity in the Little Things

Be mindful that the little things are the glue that hold integrity of character together. Examples of integrity in the little things are politeness and common courtesy. Good manners are an underpinning of a person of integrity. Such a person makes clean language a priority and watches the example that they set for others, especially children. A person of excellence doesn't gloat or trash talk. They are not overly competitive and they never derive pleasure or joy from the suffering or failings of others. They strive to be patient, kind and approachable. It's these simple everyday things that can really set us apart and place us in the best position to be of assistance to others. So while you are working on the big things, begin to be mindful of the little things that will surround and protect your overall integrity of character. When trying to navigate the path of integrity big or small within in our lives, it might be helpful to again remember the apostle Paul's advice to the Philippians:

....whatsoever things are true, whatsoever things are honest, whatsoever things are just, whatsoever things are pure, whatsoever things are lovely, whatsoever things are of good report; if there be any virtue, and if there be any praise, think on these things.

In this Lesson we have learned:

✓ That if we pursue integrity of character, we will become fine tuned to the spirit and blessings of God.

✓ By using the Golden Rule we can indentify areas of our lives that are in need of greater integrity. By making "change" in these areas a priority, our reward will not only be greater blessings, but lasting peace and happiness.

Making a Commitment

Finally, please commit to memory the following precept concerning integrity of character.

MEMORIZE: Personal Precept #9 - Becoming a Person of Integrity

♥ I will make becoming a person of integrity a priority and by using The Golden Rule I will find areas big and small in my life that are in need of this important quality.

Caring for the Spirit of Relationships

- *In this lesson we will focus on the health of our relationships and interactions with others. We will learn to identify the spirit that accompanies these interactions and then we will work to improve upon that spirit to create an improved atmosphere where God's presence can dwell.*

In Preparation:

- Read teaching two (pgs. 42 –51) of The Happiness Principle.
- Begin focusing on the state of your relationships and interactions with others.
- Pray for a greater understanding of the nature of the spirit of those relationships.

The health of the relationships that we maintain with others can be the greatest factor in determining lasting happiness. Caring for *the spirit* of each relationship is a cornerstone to staying well connected to Father and the blessings that He provides. In *teaching two* of *The Happiness Principle* we learn that our emotions and behaviors attract a powerful spiritual presence and that these energies can affect the people and environments around us. Again, the Bible lends some insight on the existence of this process.

In the 9th book of Luke it records that as Jesus and his disciples traveled to Jerusalem to celebrate Passover, he sent two of them ahead to Samaria to secure lodgings for the night. They returned reporting that the Samaritans had rejected them and told them that they were not welcome in their village. After they had recounted their experience, two of the disciples asked an ominous question:

[54] And when his disciples James and John saw this, they said, Lord, wilt thou that we command fire to come down from heaven, and consume them, even as Elias did?

[55] But he turned, and rebuked them, and said, Ye know not what manner of spirit ye are of.

[56] For the Son of man is not come to destroy men's lives, but to save them. And they went to another village.

> **"Create in me a clean heart, O God; and renew a right spirit within me."**
>
> **Psalms 51:10**

Through this experience Jesus teaches that the *manner of spirit we are of* will most likely determine how we will act and react in most situations. The apostles had been rejected and humiliated by the Samaritans and these negative actions had caused them to react by listening to the spirit of vengeance. No matter the situation, whether it be positive or negative we all react in one fashion or another and those reactions attract particular spiritual presences and promptings. Add other people and their reactions into the mix and managing healthy and productive relationships can be a challenge. So when dealing with others do you ever ask yourself, "What spirit am I of, right now in this moment? Is this relationship healthy? Is there a spirit here of which I should be careful?" Have you ever considered which spirit is being drawn toward those you deal with daily? Who are they and how do the tend to act, and what sort of spirit will those actions attract? Identifying the spiritual energies that surround us in our interactions with others is not only important to achieving happiness but it is critical in maintaining such joy and it's accompanying peace.

The Obvious Spirit

Identifying the spirit within most situations takes some practice. The first step to recognizing the spirit is by eliminating the obvious. There are certain people in all of our lives that act in predictable ways. You probably know them. There's that guy that is always making the inappropriate jokes and comments. While he seems to entertain some, he always embarrasses or angers others. How about the woman that complains about everything. She spreads negativity wherever she goes. The other complainers seem to enjoy her company but for most part she's a real downer. And how about that guy that always has to debate and argue with everyone, even over the smallest things? He always has to be right and most often he just leaves you feeling inadequate and bad about yourself. As you can see from these brief examples, some people consistently act in a certain manner and as a result carry a predictable spirit with them. If we will identify these usual suspects before we interact with them or if we can avoid dealing with them at all, we can guard against the behaviors and reactions that they inspire.

> *"For they that are after the flesh do mind the things of the flesh; but they that are after the Spirit the things of the Spirit."*
>
> *Romans 8:5*

Discerning the Spirit

So you get home from work after a long, trying day, and the children are screaming, your wife is on edge and dinner hasn't even been started yet. You already feel like you've reached your boiling point and after being with your family for just five minutes you are ready to explode. Now supposing that you can regain your composure for just a minute, here's a question. Do you think you might be able to accurately discern or read the spirit of this situation? And if so might you also be able to identify where that spirit is about to lead you and your family? Do you see a spirit of impatience and even contention forming in your home? And do you want to fix this problem and protect your family before it gets out of hand; or has the spirit of discontent and anger convinced you that you'll feel better if you start a fight and tell a few people off?

Now remember, if you wish to be connected to Father's spirit of peace and happiness, you must learn to get out of the habit of connecting with spiritual energies that interfere with His light and guidance. Half the battle is being wise enough to identify the spirit around you, and then the other half is being smart enough and controlled enough to act in a fashion that will diffuse the negative spirit, and reestablish an environment where Father's spirit can once again dwell. So with all of this in mind, when you walk through that door in the evening and find the spirit of your home in disarray, step back outside for a moment, take a couple of deep breaths, have a quick prayer, and then make an inspired decision to act instead of reacting. Make a plan. It might go something like this. Go inside and directly take the kids to the backyard or their rooms and get them involved in an activity that will distract them, but that will most importantly get them out of your wife's hair. Next go to her and tell her how much you love her, and then ask if there is anything you can do to help. Finally offer to go right back out and get a pizza so she doesn't have to hassle with dinner tonight. Now of course your tired and of course you most likely don't feel like doing any of this stuff, but if you really want peace in your home it's well worth it. It takes a little practice but if you will start monitoring the spirit in each situation in your life and then take appropriate action to help improve that spirit, you will be paving the way for Father's presence, not only in your life but in the lives of everyone with whom you come in contact.

Improving the Spirit

Within the previous example you can easily identify the powerful spirit of contention brewing in your home but within other situations the destructive spirit may be more subtle. In time you will be able to discern the most cunning of spiritual influences with a little practice and an increased awareness. Again as demonstrated in our example, the second half of the process is getting to work improving the spirit that you have identified. This too takes practice and most importantly, inspiration but once you have developed this spiritual skill, you will find yourself in possession of something extremely valuable. You will find yourself in a position to help change negative spiritual environments into ones that are more positive and uplifting. It might be in an instant or it may take some time, but your example, your words, your very presence and the soothing spirit that accompanies you will heal the spiritual environment around you, not just for your benefit but to the benefit of everyone with whom you associate. You will be a vehicle for change. Through you fear will be changed to courage, doubt will be changed to hope, discontent to gratitude, and contention to peace. Any environment that is in spiritual disorder will benefit from Father's spirit of love and peace that will flow through you. You will be a peacemaker.

Becoming a Peacemaker

In the 5th chapter of Matthew during His Sermon on the Mount, Jesus makes an interesting reference to peace:

[9] *Blessed are the peacemakers: for they shall be called the children of God.*

Here He refers to a person known as a *peacemaker*, and He tells us that these people will be known as *the children of God*. Now over the years God has been referred to by many names, but His highest and most revered title is simply *Father*. So the highest title that we can hold in this life or the next is the title *child of God*. It is through this high position as true *children of God* that we will make the greatest connection with Him and the lasting happiness that He has to offer. So becoming a peacemaker is another important part of making this connection.

So what is a peacemaker? Is it a person that mediates or acts as a referee between people who are having issues with each other? Well in a sense but there is much more to it, especially in the sense that Jesus is referring. A peacemaker is someone who works to change the spiritual environment from one that is spiritually toxic to one in which God's spirit can dwell uninterrupted or in other words, one of peace. It is a person who tries to identify destructive spiritual influence in most situations and instead of participating with it, works to overcome it. It is someone that is always working on positive personal development so that they might be a clean pathway for God's powerful and loving spirit; a conduit through which His spirit can positively overwhelm any negative situation. So by striving to learn how to become a *peacemaker*, we earn the title of *children of God*, and place ourselves and our families in the position to receive His greatest favor and most rich blessings.

Here's an IDEA:

⇒ Let's start identifying the spirit that is carried by the people around us. On a piece of paper list at least five of the people with whom you closely associate. Next list at least three examples of the spiritual tendencies that that each carry with them. Keep this list confidential so as to not hurt anyone's feelings, but start becoming consciously acquainted with the presence the surrounds others so that you might help them and yourself operate in an increasing place of peace in the future.

Learning to Make Peace

In the following exercise that we call "Making Peace", we will begin to learn how to become peacemakers in many of life's situations. Whether it is a certain person or situation, we will learn how to analyze these encounters after they have happened so that we might better deal with them in the future. By looking back at these instances and learning from them, in time you will learn to act differently when in these environments and follow God's spirit and promptings, instead of the prevailing disruptive spirit. It is through such practice that in time you'll become a maker of peace. The following are the steps to this process:

1)   Indentifying a person or situation with a disruptive spirit.

It's important to understand that a *disruptive spirit* is one that interferes with the peaceful spirit that is necessary for God's influence to flow and be heard. It is not necessarily an obvious and outwardly destructive spirit such as anger or contention, but it can be something as seemingly innocent or harmless as someone who brags a lot, or a person that regularly speaks to others in a demeaning or impatient tone. It may not be a particular person but it might

> *"For God hath not given us the spirit of fear; but of power, and of love, and of a sound mind."*
>
> *2 Timothy 1:7*

be a situation in which you find yourself regularly. For example you might feel that people take advantage of you regularly, whether you know them well or not. It could be a one time situation that you need to analyze such as a contentious moment of road rage on the way home from work. While it would be impossible to itemize every type of disruptive spirit, the following list might aid in helping you label these influences with yourself and others.

• Rude	• Untrustworthy	• Demeaning	• Envious	• Dishonest
• Domineering	• Disrespectful	• Controlling	• Stubborn	• Gossiping
• Selfish	• Judgmental	• Ungrateful	• Jealous	• Contentious
• Inconsiderate	• Impatient	• Lying	• Unkind	• Hateful

2)   How does this disruptive spirit make you feel?

In the 4th chapter of 1st John, the apostle encourages us to test these spirits when he says:

[1] Beloved, believe not every spirit, but try the spirits whether they are of God:

Now that you have labeled the spirit, it is now time to try or test it. How did it inspire you to act or react? At this point we are not interested in how you actually reacted but in how you felt and what you wanted to do. Focus upon not only how you felt in the moment but how you continued to feel after the event was over. The reason we separate how you felt from how you actually acted is to see what kinds of spiritual promptings you are hearing in these moments. Again maybe you feel taken advantage of in a certain situation and you wanted to fight back and say something rude but you didn't feel like you had the courage. For another person such a situation might make them feel vulnerable and unable to respond and at a loss as to what to do.

Next, ask yourself this question: If this disruptive spirit could speak, what would it say to you? What might it encourage you to do in that moment? If it is an angry spirit then it would probably want you to also become angry. If it is fearful in nature then creating fear within you would probably be the goal, and if it is a spirit of gossip, then it would greatly desire that you also talk behind the backs of others and spread its rumors. Of course a disruptive spirit doesn't always encourage a "like" response. For instance a domineering spirit usually inspires submission in its target or a jealous spirit most often promotes guilt.

"Now the Spirit speaketh expressly, that in the latter times some shall depart from the faith, giving heed to seducing spirits "

1 Timothy 4:1

3)   *How are you participating with this disruptive spirit?*

So now that you have tried the spirit and have identified how it made you feel and how you wanted to react, and the nature of the disruptive spirit; it's time to ask yourself the following questions: Did you follow the promptings of this disruptive spirit? Did you participate with it and if so how? It's important to keep in mind that you are not being accused. We all participate with disruptive spirits from time to time; it's part of the human condition. You should try to be as analytical and dispassionate as possible here. This can be hard to do with a subject so filled with emotion and passion but don't take it personally; were trying to learn and overcome at this point. If you find that you reacted in any negative or disruptive fashion, or directly participated with the spirit then you've got some work to do. If you were "still" or used a peaceful and controlled response and didn't react or participate then you are probably in a better position for change. Remember it is our goal to add to the peace not take from it. You are not being asked to be taken advantage of but perhaps to come up with a new approach that keeps you from participating with the prevailing disruptive spirit and that will put you in a better position to receive God's guidance and be a vehicle for his peace and healing spirit.

4)   *What is your plan to overcome this disruptive spirit?*

Next we need to make a plan to improve our approach to dealing with such a person or situation in the future. Just because your current response was peaceful or non-confrontational doesn't mean that there isn't room for improvement. For instance, if you are dealing with someone who is belittling and demeaning, just being quiet and taking it is not a complete peace-making answer. While this approach is preferable to becoming combative and contentious, if in the end you are left feeling humiliated and depressed, you will not be a good conduit for God's spirit and his power for change. During this phase of the process you should turn to Father in prayer and ask for his help and guidance in formulating a plan. One approach might be to go to the person in private and in a positive and non-confrontational manner, share with them how their interactions make you feel. You might tell them that you value them and that you would like to have a better relationship with them, but that these negative interactions are standing in the way of that. If this doesn't seem like a reasonable approach, perhaps you could go to other people that regularly associate with this person. See if they won't encourage them to be kinder and more thoughtful especially in the moment that it is happening. Perhaps when it happens again you could try harder to not react to the negative but be more proactively positive and uplifting in your conversation and overwhelm the situation with Father's light. Whatever your course of action, be sure to pray upon it and ponder upon it and try to get in touch with God's plan concerning it. This process takes some work and it can be tricky so you are encouraged to enlist some outside help. Your HP Guide should know you, your life and your relationships pretty well at this point and they should be able to help you identify area's that need work and to develop a plan to help improve them.

EXERCISE: Making Peace

♦ Here is your chance to begin your journey towards becoming a peacemaker. On a separate piece of paper outline the four steps of making piece. 1) Choose a person or type of situation that recurs in your life, that tends to carry a disruptive spirit and then label that spirit. 2) Test the spirit by outlining how it makes you feel and what it's prompting you to do. 3) Detail how you actually reacted to this disruptive spirit and what it inspired you to say and do. 4) Finally, formulate a plan to better deal with this disruptive spirit and get to work adding more of God's peace to such situations in the future. Have your HP Guide help you with this exercise.

Inspiring the Spirit

Of course one of the most important parts of monitoring the spirit in any situation is too stay aware of the spirit that we carry with ourselves. Keep in mind that we cannot be peace keepers if we are the ones that initiate the disruptive spirit within our relationships. Now everyone should be allowed to have a bad day here and there, but as peacemakers we need to consistently try to carry a good and uplifting spirit into every situation.

In this Lesson we have learned:

✓ That our relationships and interactions with others can carry with them powerful disruptive spiritual energies that can interfere with God's influence and blessings.

✓ We must identify and label these disruptive spirits and how we tend to react to their influence. We must then formulate and apply a plan to overcoming them permanently.

Making a Commitment

Finally, please commit to memory the following precept concerning caring for the spirit of relationships.

MEMORIZE: Personal Precept #10 - Caring for the Spirit of Relationships

♥ I will try to identify and improve upon the spirit of most situations and every relationship so that God's presence will be free to heal and bless the world around me.

www.ingramcontent.com/pod-product-compliance
Lightning Source LLC
Chambersburg PA
CBHW052342100426

42736CB00047B/3435